Lorenzo Burge

Aryas, Semites and Jews

Lorenzo Burge

Aryas, Semites and Jews

ISBN/EAN: 9783337148355

Printed in Europe, USA, Canada, Australia, Japan

Cover: Foto ©ninafisch / pixelio.de

More available books at **www.hansebooks.com**

ARYAS, SEMITES AND JEWS

JEHOVAH AND THE CHRIST

.... A RECORD OF SPIRITUAL ADVANCE FROM THE HOUSEHOLD OR PERSONAL GOD OF THE SEMITE ABRAM, AND FROM JEHOVAH, THE TUTELARY OR NATIONAL GOD OF THE ISRAELITES, TO THE UNIVERSAL FATHER REVEALED BY JESUS THE CHRIST: WITH THE CONTRACTS MADE BETWEEN THE HOUSEHOLD GOD AND ABRAM; THE TUTELARY GOD, JEHOVAH AND THE ISRAELITES; AND BETWEEN OUR FATHER IN HEAVEN AND ALL MANKIND.... ALSO THE CIRCUMSTANCES, INCIDENTS, AND EVENTS ATTENDING THE PREPARATION FOR AND THE PROMULGATION OF THE SECOND REVELATION....................

By LORENZO BURGE

AUTHOR OF "PRE-GLACIAL MAN, AND THE ARYAN RACE"

PUBLISHED A.D. 1889

BY LEE AND SHEPARD, 10 MILK STREET, BOSTON, NEXT "THE OLD SOUTH MEETINGHOUSE," AND CAN BE HAD OF ALL RESPECTABLE BOOK-DEALERS, OR SAID BOOK WILL BE SENT BY MAIL UPON RECEIPT OF THE PRICE, $1.50....

COPYRIGHT, 1888,
BY LORENZO BURGE.

All rights reserved.

ARYAS, SEMITES AND JEWS.

BOSTON
S. J. PARKHILL & CO. PRINTERS

"God is love; and he that dwelleth in love dwelleth in God, and God in him." — 1 John iv. 16.

"If any man say, I love God, and hateth his brother, he is a liar." — 1 John iv. 20.

"And this commandment have we from him, That he who loveth God love his brother also." — 1 John iv. 21.

"Whoso hath this world's good, and seeth his brother have need, and shutteth up his bowels of compassion from him, how dwelleth the love of God in him?" — 1 John iii. 17.

"No man cometh unto the Father, but by me." — John xiv. 6.

"Jesus Christ of Nazareth, whom ye crucified, whom God raised from the dead. . . . This is the stone which was set at nought of you builders, which is become the head of the corner. Neither is there salvation in any other: for there is none other name under heaven given among men, whereby we must be saved." — Acts iv. 10, 11, 12.

"Other foundation can no man lay than that is laid, which is Jesus Christ." — 1 Cor. iii. 11.

PREFACE.

In our previous volume, "Pre-Glacial Man and the Aryan Race," speaking of the history revealed in the early chapters of Genesis, we said, "Great as is the value of this history, it has been preserved merely as a vehicle in which to transmit a record of the first revelation made by the Deity to man through the Aryan race; the duty laid upon that race to promulgate it; their neglect of that duty, and their consequent removal by God from the civilized world."

In this volume we propose to resume the thread of history, and show the movements of the Deity in the selection of a people through whom, in the fulness of time, men should be sufficiently enlightened to receive, and from whom that being should proceed, who, as God's messenger, should again give to man, that revelation before given to the Aryas and rejected.

In the volume mentioned, we have the record of the revelation made to the Aryan race, with the injunction to spread the knowledge throughout the world. We have seen that race neglect the opportunities granted them to perform that duty; the consequent destruction of their nation; the banishment of the race; their relapse into barbarism; and the loss to the world of the first revelation.

After some two thousand or twenty-five hundred years, during which the Turanian, Hamite, and Semitic races kept alive the civilization and knowledge received by them from the Aryas, the Deity, who was at that time unknown to man, took measures to again reveal himself; and in the Bible is the record of his work. In this book we find a nearly continuous history of the Hebrew nation, and it also contains a record of their spiritual progress.

Unwittingly, the writers have given us the means of tracing every movement of the Deity, until He for whose advent the nation itself was created, and to prepare for whose coming all this work had been performed, — he, the Christ, appeared; and through him, the Deity, his law and requirements, were again made known, and again placed in the hands of the Aryas, with a repetition of the former injunction to promulgate it throughout the world.

The Christian religion has long been overburdened by the belief that the Bible is one book, all parts equal in importance, and all the product of direct inspiration from the Deity.

This belief has caused the simple and direct teachings of Jesus, the Christ, to be covered and hidden by crude dogmas, drawn by ignorance and superstition from the old, barbarous, and cruel record of the dealings of Jehovah, the tutelary god of the Hebrews, with that nation; until Christianity (so called) has become an instrument for clothing our loving and dear Father in heaven with the garb of, and for ascribing to him the characteristics of, the outgrown and dead Jehovah. The Jewish nation is dead; and the god of that nation died, *as Jehovah,* with it.

In the hope that Christian teachers and people may be brought to see the folly and crime of such teaching, I place this book in their hands, trusting it may remove the scales of superstition and bigotry from their eyes, and that they may see the beauty, the power, the loveliness, the simplicity, of the teachings of the Christ, the anointed and authorized messenger of our Father in heaven.

In our main work we have quoted freely from the New Testament, to show the identity of the Christ's teachings with the original. Incident thereto, we have exposed the prevalence of false Christianity, and have revealed the second coming of the Christ.

CONTENTS.

CHAPTER		PAGE
I.	THE INTERREGNUM	11
II.	THE HEBREWS	21
	ABRAHAM, ISAAC, AND JACOB, AND THEIR HOUSEHOLD GOD	21
	MOSES, THE ISRAELITES, AND JEHOVAH THEIR TUTELARY OR NATIONAL GOD	33
III.	THE JEWS	53
	CYRUS TO THE CHRIST	53
	ANNO DOMINI	66
	JESUS THE CHRIST	72
IV.	THE CLAIM OF JESUS OF NAZARETH TO BE THE CHRIST	87
	MESSIANIC PROPHECIES	90
	JESUS OF NAZARETH	96
	THE CHRIST	102
	THE SON OF GOD	104
	CORROBORATIVE TESTIMONY	113
	SON OF MAN	117
	OTHER TESTIMONY	122
	THE CHRIST'S MIRACLES	127
	PRE-EXISTENCE	133
V.	THE FIRST AND SECOND REVELATIONS COMPARED	140
	ONE GOD	140
	THE LOVE OF GOD	148

CHAPTER		PAGE
	THE KINGDOM OF HEAVEN	154
	GOD OUR FATHER	160
	ETERNAL LIFE THE GIFT OF GOD	167
	GOD'S PLAN OF SALVATION	178
	ETERNAL DEATH, OR DISSOLUTION	184
VI.	OTHER CHRISTIAN SUBJECTS	200
	ANGELS AND DEVILS, HEAVEN AND HELL	200
	MIRACLES	210
	THE CRUCIFIXION	216
	THE RESURRECTION	229
	THE DISCIPLES	237
	THE APOSTLES	243
	THE SECOND COMING OF THE CHRIST	256
	THE CHRIST AN ENIGMA	262
	THE HOLY SPIRIT IN THE NINETEENTH CENTURY	268
	FALSE CHRISTIANITY	272
	LOYALTY TO GOD	283
	THE SECOND GARDEN OF EDEN	288
	THE COMPLETION OF THE SECOND REVELATION, AND THE END OF THE JEWISH NATION	294
	THE ESSENTIALS OF CHRISTIANITY	297

APPENDIX:
    EARLY CIVILIZATION IN THE EUPHRATES VALLEY 299

ARYAS, SEMITES AND JEWS.

I.

THE INTERREGNUM.

IN our former volume, we followed the fortunes of the Aryas to the period of their extinction as a nation, and their final dispersion, which we are informed was in the time of, or at the birth of, Peleg, B. C. 2247 by the Bible chronology, but by the enlarged chronology caused by Assyrian discoveries, which we have adopted in our previous volume, some two thousand years earlier; viz., B.C. 4304. Bible chronology places the birth of Abram, during the reign of the Semites, at B.C. 2056. In the Bible we have no account of the events transpiring during this interregnum of 2,248 years, and we can only look to Assyria or Egypt to enlighten the darkness.[1]

[1] In the appendix we give quotations from the writings of Professors Smith, Sayce, and other Assyriologists, showing the high state of civilization of the Semitic occupants of the Euphrates Valley at the time of Sargon I., B.C. 3800, and the consequent civilization of the original occupants of the valley thousands of years before.

Some four hundred years previous to the dispersion of the remnant of the Aryas, the Flood had overwhelmed and destroyed the Aryan nation, which were then occupying the Euphrates Valley and the borders of the Persian Gulf. The destruction of this nation cut off from the Aryan rulers of Egypt their source of supply for their army; and they were in no condition to successfully withstand the uprising of the Egyptians under a native prince or leader, who, some time after the Deluge, vanquished and drove from their country the foreign race that had for so long a time ruled over them.

B.C. 3800, we find Sargon I., a Semite, ruling over the country. The Turanian language had become obsolete; and he caused a collection to be made of the numerous religious and scientific books, astronomical and astrological works, histories, and other books written in the Turanian tongue, and appointed learned men to translate them into the vernacular. He also caused dictionaries, grammars, and phrase-books to be written, that the knowledge contained in these old books might not be lost. Through the work of this enlightened sovereign it is that Assyriologists are enabled to gain a knowledge of the Turanian language, and thus transcribe some of the earliest cylinders.

While the early Turanians were undoubtedly aware of the previous rule of the Aryas over Asia, and of their destruction by the Flood, these facts would hardly appear in their national records, as they would form no part of *their* history. In course of time, having no interest in them, the whole subject would be forgotten, or become matter of tradition.

The Semites would take but little interest in the Turanian traditions respecting the Aryas, if they were aware of any. With them, the origin of civilization and learning had taken the form of myth, and the original meaning was forgotten. The allegory of the creation, Adam and Eve, and the deluge, was kept intact, and was treasured by them as a literal record of facts. In their popular writings they naturally introduced the names of their own gods as the actors; as, long afterward, the Hebrews did the same in part, giving to their god, Jehovah, the credit of the creation of man, and the causing of the deluge.

The fact that such a people as the Aryas should have existed, and ruled over Southern Central Asia for five thousand years, and yet the record of their existence be so completely lost that only the legend of the "Oannes" remained to indicate their work of civilization, is remarkable and strange. It must have required a long period of time, and many changes, to have so entirely obliterated such an existence, and leave in utter oblivion the nation which philology proves to have been the progenitor of the present most civilized races of mankind.

The slow progress of two or three thousand years, the intervention of these two alien races, their long reigns, and the entire disappearance of the Aryas, caused their history to die out of the memory of man. Excepting the Oannes myth, not even a legend of them remained to attest their former existence, until, in the providence of God, the hidden records in the allegory were brought forth, and God's work and requirements made known.[1]

In "Pre-Glacial Man" we have seen the intentions of God apparently thwarted. The race to whom he had intrusted a knowledge of himself,

---

[1] In Professor Sayce's "Fresh Light from the Ancient Monuments," we obtain some knowledge of another ancient nation, the Hittites, whose history had been lost to the world, except in the incident of the purchase by Abraham of the cave of Machpelah, and in the slight mention of them among the Canaanitish nations occupying Canaan at the time of the Hebrew exodus. The monuments lately discovered show them to have reigned over a territory extending from the Mediterranean to the Euphrates, and from Egypt to Northern Syria. For many hundreds of years they ruled this region on terms of equality with Egypt on the south, and Assyria on the east: yet, until these discoveries, their former existence as a powerful nation was unknown.

his laws and requirements, and of the immortal destiny of man, with the command that they should spread abroad this knowledge, and teach it to all mankind, had been false to its trust, and had neglected to fulfil its obligations.

The main body of the race had deteriorated, had become debased and vile, and by the hand of God had been swept from the face of the earth; while the remainder were occupying portions of Western Asia, and Europe, far from the centres of civilization and knowledge. They had become the savage, uncivilized portion of the human race; and the Semites, one of the before-despised barbarian races, had become rulers of Central Asia, and the inheritors of the arts, science, culture, and civilization of the world.

In Egypt, one of the great centres of civilization, the native Egyptian race were ruled over by the Hyksos, a foreign race of shepherd-kings, who had conquered them one or two hundred years before. These Hyksos were undoubtedly a portion of the Semitic inhabitants of the Euphrates Valley, who had overrun and now ruled over the Egyptians.

The revelation made to the Aryas having thus been lost to the world, after a lapse of two thousand years or more God again prepares to make himself known to man.

Before attempting to trace the movements of the Deity in carrying out his purpose, we will endeavor to ascertain the physical, moral, and spiritual condition of the world, as exhibited in the ruling races of mankind at that period.

Away back three thousand years or more, a branch of the Aryan race had held sway for eight hundred or a thousand years over these same Egyptians. The evidence of this foreign rule was shown in the advance made in some of the arts and sciences, and in a trace of the religion of the Aryas shown in the doctrine taught to the priests of a spiritual and invisible God who ruled the universe, and in the introduction into their own religion, of a system of future reward for the good and of punishment for the wicked in the world beyond.

The religion of the Egyptians was otherwise of the very lowest description. They worshipped various gods, whom they supposed had power over the seasons, the crops, the insect and other plagues, and over the various powers of nature, with Osiris as their supreme god, and Isis his wife. They also held many animals as sacred, and sacrificed to them. While the priests and a few of the learned men held more enlightened views, the people generally were sunk in the darkest spiritual ignorance. In the arts and sciences of civilization, they were far advanced, in fact, leading the world in intellectual knowledge, and in material power and riches; having vast armies and navies, and holding commerce with Europe and the Indies.

The Euphrates Valley, the other centre of civilization, was inhabited by the Semitic race. In absorbing the arts, science, and civilization of the Turanians, who had preceded them, they had, with the civilization, also adopted their religious beliefs; and we find here a religion in some respects higher than that of Egypt, yet still of a very low order.

They worshipped gods innumerable. Heaven, earth, and sea, each had its god. Every city had its tutelary god; and every house its teraphim, or household god. The Deity was unknown, and his powers and attributes had been distributed among the thousand and one gods of nature.

Under these circumstances, how could a knowledge of the Deity, his laws and requirements, be revealed to man? The spiritual nature of the Semites had not been unfolded. This earth bounded their views. The idea of one God, the maker and sustainer of the universe, the father and lover of mankind, was too vast, and entirely beyond their comprehension.

The Aryan race had been naturally of a higher

type, a more spiritual race; in their early experience, they had been entirely secluded from all other nations. As the leading and most advanced race, they had received from God a gradual revelation; their minds were fallow, and open to receive such spiritual instruction as might be vouchsafed; and they had no pre-conceived ideas of God, or of the powers of nature, to be overcome. They had, consequently, received the first evangel pure and undefiled by man's devices.

But the Semites were a race whose spiritual nature was as yet unawakened. Enterprising, ambitious, selfish, and cruel; desiring and working for temporal wealth; their thoughts limited to this world and their creature comforts, — how were they to be enlightened, and, through them, the world receive a knowledge of spiritual things?

If the Deity had sent a messenger to proclaim his being and power to the Semites, he would not have been received. They had already gods of the heavens and the earth, whose powers were unquestioned. What could the new deity do more than they? If received at all, he would have been only as one among many gods.

Apparently, the Deity could only introduce himself to mankind by creating a race or nation who knew no god; who should be secluded and gradually instructed, as were the Aryas of old, until they should reach a height of intelligence which would enable them to receive the proposed revelation.

In the Old Testament, we can see what was done by the Deity. In the record made by the Hebrews themselves (a portion of the Semite race), we can trace every step taken by God toward the promulgation of the second revelation.

What God determined to do, is shown by what he did do. In selecting an individual from the Semitic or Semite race as the progenitor or father of the people or nation who should be the instrument in his hands, again to give to man the revelation once given to the Aryas, but now lost and forgotten, the Deity must work with a race of duller spiritual perceptions, and one in every way inferior to the Aryas, whose work they will be called upon in part to perform. They are of the earth earthy in their nature. This earth bounds their views: only through their senses can they be taught. They must have an object to worship which can be recognized by the senses.

As an inducement to right living, worldly blessings must be promised; and sickness, plague, famine, and war be threatened as consequent on evil-doing.

It took five thousand years for the Aryas to reach the height of their spiritual knowledge; but this people will not, can not reach that point at all. They will not be required to spread the knowledge of God throughout the world: that is the duty resting on the Aryas. This people will merely be required to prepare the way, and produce the man who shall in God's good time, through special instruction and inspiration, again give unto the Aryas the revelation which, once their own, was for a time taken from them because of disobedience and neglect of its requirements.

The first step in the long progress of events was the selection of Abram, a Semite inhabitant of the city of Ur, a city in what was afterward known as Southern Babylonia.

II.

THE HEBREWS.

ABRAHAM, ISAAC, AND JACOB, AND THEIR HOUSEHOLD GOD.

FROM the Hebrew Scriptures we learn that Abram was a citizen of Ur, one of the oldest of the Chaldæan cities. From the cylinders we find that at the time of his birth that city was at the height of its prosperity, and was the principal or capital city of the southern district of the country afterward known as Babylonia.

Its name "Ur" comes from the tutelary god worshipped by its inhabitants, the moon; and Ur means the moon-city. It was situate about six miles west of the Euphrates, perhaps ten or twenty miles from its mouth. The rivers Tigris and Euphrates bring down each year so much sediment, that the land rapidly encroaches on the Persian Gulf; and the present mouth of the Euphrates is many miles beyond the outlet of the river at the time of Abram.[1]

---

[1] The ruins of Ur, now known as Mugheir, show that it was originally surrounded by a wall, and was a place of considerable importance. The first monarch of Ur, whose name has been

Terah, the father of Abram, the Scriptures inform us, "was a worshipper of other gods," and Hebrew traditions call him a maker of images or teraphim.

Teraphim were images of the household gods, made of any size, some small to be easily carried on a journey, and others of life size. Kitto's Cyclopædia says, "They were similar to the 'Penates;'" and calls them "tutelar household gods, by whom families expected, for worship bestowed, to be rewarded with domestic prosperity, such as plenty of food, health, and the various necessaries of domestic life."

In Genesis it is stated, that Rachel, the wife of Jacob, secreted her father Laban's images, or teraphim; and Laban, in his interview with Jacob, charges him with having "stolen his gods." When Jacob goes to Bethel, at the command of his god, he orders his household to "put away the strange gods that are among you," evidently referring to images or teraphim. In Judges, Micah, it is stated, "made an ephod, and teraphim," for the purpose of worship. These household gods

---

preserved, is Lig-Bagus, wno ruled apparently a little before the time of Abram. He extended his empire by conquest over most of Southern Babylonia. At Ur, he built a temple to the moon-god, a tower, and a palace; remains of the temple still exist. He also erected a temple in Larsa; one to the god Anu, in Erech; and one to Bel, at Nipur.

were well known to the Israelites, both before and after Moses.

To understand the Bible account of Abram, we must first know what were the influences surrounding him during his sixty years' residence in Ur, previous to his removal with his father Terah. This knowledge we obtain from the Babylonian cylinders.

The Semites in the Euphrates Valley, as we have before said, were worshippers of many gods. The whole universe was divided up among them. Anu was the supreme ruler of the heavens, and had command over the seven baleful spirits of the air, or winds. Bel, or Belus, the Baal of Scripture, was god of the middle region; he represented the principle of active and creative life, and held sway on earth. Hea governed the regions under the earth, and the sea. The throne-bearers, or seven wicked spirits of the sea, were under his control. Hea was also the representative of wisdom. Vul, the son of Anu, was the god of the atmosphere and its phenomena. Anatu, the wife of Anu, was goddess of life and death. Istar, daughter of Anu, afterward known as Astarte or Venus, and in Scripture as Ashtoreth, represented the heavenly bodies. She is also portrayed as the mother of mankind, and as the goddess of licentious love. Elu, prince of gods, was the principal god of war, and is afterward known as Mars. Nagal was also a war-god. Shamus was the sun-god. Merodach was benefactor of mankind; Maklin, god of dreams; with many others of less note, also tutelary gods of the various cities and villages, down to the tutelar household gods. A change of rulers frequently caused a change in the god worshipped in the city or country. The same was true of the household god. Those old Babylonians believed that the gods desired sacrifice; the burning of fragrant woods and the flavors of burning flesh were grateful to them, and they would flock in crowds to smell the sacrifice. The Bible says of the sacrifice of Noah, "and the Lord smelled a sweet savor;" and the Babylonian legend, speaking of the same thing, says, "The gods collected at its burning; the gods like flies over the sacrifice gathered." In return for this sacrifice (which was not an act of worship as we understand it, but merely an offering for benefits received or expected), the god to whom the sacrifice was offered, it was believed, would protect, care for, and aid the worshipper in his undertakings, and give him health, food, and success. If the worshipper did not succeed, he became dissatisfied with his god, and unceremoniously dethroned him as weak and powerless, and put in his place another, and, as he hoped, a more powerful deity.

They had no fear, love, or reverence for them: they were merely convenient helpers.

The supreme god Anu, with Bel, god of earth, and Hea, god of the sea, they believed to have been created by the forces of nature; with the exception of these and their immediate descendants, they believed the gods to have been men, who, for services rendered on earth, had been made immortal. By thus becoming immortal, they had obtained and wielded power beyond that of man, and became gods.

In the Book of Acts, we read that the inhabitants of Lystra desired to offer sacrifice to Barnabas and Paul, as being Jupiter and Mercury. After the shipwreck at Melita, Paul shook off the viper that had fastened on his hand, without injury; and they said, "He is a god." The Lares and Penates are the same as the household gods of Abram's time; and a Christian adaptation of the same belief is seen in Europe in the Roman-Catholic worship of saints.

The duties of the household god, in return for sacrificial offerings, are expressed in the covenant or bargain made by Jacob with his god as recorded in Genesis: —

"Jacob vowed a vow, saying, If God will be with me, and will keep me in this way that I go, and will give me bread to eat, and raiment to put on, so that I come again to my father's house in peace, then shall the Lord be my Lord."

This illustrates the belief and the expectation of the men of those times, and shows the nature of the covenant or bargain made between the parties. In payment for this care and these blessings, Jacob promises the usual sacrifice. "Of all thou shalt give me, I will surely give the tenth unto thee:" in other words, will spend that amount in incense and sacrifices.[1]

We smile at the Eastern legends and traditions respecting Abraham: yet Christians have fallen into as great a misconception of his character, by imagining that the god with whom he covenanted and conversed was the Deity as revealed by the Christ two thousand years later. Jehovah, the Hebrew tutelary god revealed by Moses; and our Father, revealed by the Christ, — were both alike unknown to Abraham.

Then, who and what was the god revealed to Abram? and what does the Scripture story mean?

Abram for sixty years was a resident of Ur. He was in no way different from the other inhabitants of the city. Like them he was a believer

---

[1] Undoubtedly, most Christians in their early manhood would gladly make an agreement to give ten per cent of their income to the support of religion or to charity, upon a contract like the above. Yet how few from their incomes pay to the Giver any such proportion!

in, and a worshipper of, the gods of Babylonia: he knew no others. At sixty years of age he journeyed to Haran with his father, who took with him his gods; and there the family remained until the death of Terah.

Previous to this time, Abram had received this message, as he believed, from a household god: "I will make of thee a great nation, and I will bless thee, and make thy name great, and thou shalt be a blessing; and I will bless them that bless thee, and curse him that curseth thee; and in thee shall all the families of the earth be blessed." This was the promise. The consideration for all these blessings was, "Get thee out of thy country, and from thy kindred, and from thy father's house, unto a land that I will show thee."

We see that he did not do this until his father's death; then "Abram departed, . . . and they went forth into the land of Canaan." Abram showed that he had faith in the promise, by fulfilling the condition; and this was the first step in the contract made between Abram, and the Deity in the character of a household god.

A revelation such as was afterward made through the Christ could not have been understood by the Semites at that time, neither were they far enough advanced at the time of Moses. God reveals himself to the extent of the ability of man to receive. For eighteen hundred years *we* have had the Christ's revelation; yet how few Christians have the ability to receive it to-day!

To reach or influence man, the only way open was for the Deity to meet man on his own plane of knowledge and belief, crude as it was, and through that belief carry forward his own objects; and that is what he did do.

Abram believed that his worship of a household god made it obligatory on the part of that god to help him. He received the proposition of the god naturally, and showed his faith in the message by removing to the land pointed out. That was the first step, and fulfilled his part of the agreement or covenant.

Abram's obedience received its reward by a visible or personal appearance, and he was encouraged by a promise of a gift of the land to his seed. In answer Abram erected an altar on the plain of Moreh and afterward at Bethel, and offered sacrifice to this god; this was equal to a vow of confidence. From thence he travelled to Egypt, where he was protected by his god; and he returned to Bethel laden with riches. In return for this protection and increase, he called upon the name of, or sacrificed to, his god.

At a later period the promise was made more particular in its terms, and stronger; and the promised protection was soon put to the test in his conflict with Chedorlaomer and the allied kings, in which he won the battle, and rescued Lot from bondage. On his return he was met by Melchizedek, who informed him that he had conquered Chedorlaomer by the aid of "the most high God, possessor of heaven and earth." This was the first knowledge Abram had received as to the personality or position of the god whom he served; and he immediately gave the credit of his success to the "most high God, possessor of heaven and earth," in his response to the king of Sodom. Every god previously known to Abram had a name, but as yet he did not know the name of the god he served.

After these things, Abram was still more strengthened by the promise, "Fear not, Abram: I am thy shield, and thy exceeding great reward," and with the additional promise of a son, and that his seed should be in number as the stars in heaven. Then comes the dream, in which the servitude of the Hebrews was foretold, and the result; and a covenant, or agreement of possession, was made with Abram. We see that the promises of the god were continually enlarged, and Abram was prospered in all his undertakings. Coming in contact with the king of Egypt, it was Abram's god who was known and acknowledged.

Thus the Deity endeavored to enlarge Abram's idea of his power, and to strengthen his confidence in him.

When Abram was ninety-nine years old, his god, as he believed, appeared unto him, and revealed himself as the "Almighty God," and talked with him; changed his name to Abraham, and established with him the covenant of circumcision; and "he and all the men of his house were circumcised the same day." Shortly after, Abraham held an argument with a being who he believed was his god, relative to the destruction of the cities of the plain.

In all these interviews, in which God is represented as appearing in the form of a man, and holding intercourse, face to face, with Abraham, we must remember what Abraham's belief was. A man who had become immortal was to him a god. He would meet one, so immortalized into a god, on a plane of equality. The exhibition of any extraordinary power by a being in human form would lead Abraham to believe in him as a god, — as did the Grecians long years afterward; and as did Jacob, when he wrestled all night with a man, who then, with a touch of his finger, put out his thigh-joint; and Jacob said, "I have seen God face to face, and my life is preserved." At a later time, the Deity said unto Moses, speaking of

Aaron, "Thou shalt be to him instead of God;" also of Pharaoh, "I have made thee a god to Pharaoh." Thus we see any unusual appearance, or the possession of extraordinary power, led to the belief that the possessor was a god; and it is this belief which is expressed in the words and acts of Abraham; and they make true the statement of Christ, "No man hath seen God at any time."

The contract or covenant of circumcision was continued with Isaac, and renewed with Jacob. God had been revealed to them, also, as the Almighty; but they do not seem to have given any thought to its meaning, and do not give him his title. He is known to their descendants simply as a personal or household god, as "their fathers' god," or "the god of Abraham, Isaac, and Jacob."

The various experiences of the patriarchs, and the power shown in their behalf by this household god, gave him a place in the worship of their descendants; and we find the acknowledgment of it down to the days of servitude to the Egyptians.

Various events caused the children of Jacob, with their father, to settle in Egypt, a portion of the country being assigned to them as their residence.

After the death of Jacob, several hundred years passed. In the changes of rulers, the former honored guests had become the bondmen of Egypt. The belief in the power and personal care of their fathers' god had, during their long years of servitude, died out. Some still remembered there was a god of Abraham, Isaac, and Jacob; but they had lost all faith in his power. If he had at one time been " possessor of heaven and earth," as he claimed, he evidently had lost his power on the earth. Had he not led them into captivity, and then deserted them? Had they not besought his help, until they had ceased in despair? The large promises made to their fathers had not been fulfilled, and apparently would not be. The God of Abraham, Isaac, and Jacob was powerless, and his promises of no avail. For hundreds of years they had been bondmen, and no help had come to them; and they had long ceased to expect it. The mighty gods of Egypt had proved to be too powerful for this household god, and they had no refuge.

The descendants of Abraham had increased to millions. A nation, in numbers, had been formed, and kept separate from all other nations by the peculiarity of their position. The Deity had dealt with the patriarchs as a household god. He had obtained their full and unwavering faith by fulfilling his promises to them, but their descendants knew him not.

MOSES, THE ISRAELITES, AND JEHOVAH THEIR TUTELARY OR NATIONAL GOD.

It is under these circumstances that the Deity takes another step in the accomplishment of his purpose. Moses is brought forward as a messenger from this god who has been so long silent and unobservant of their misery.

Up to this time, Moses' life had been an exceptional one. Adopted and brought up by the Egyptian queen, he had received a thorough schooling in the religion of the Egyptians, and had been a worshipper of their gods. He was aware of the sufferings of his race; at one time, in the heat of his indignation, he had killed an Egyptian in defence of a Hebrew, and had been obliged to flee on account of it. We may suppose that at this time he was conversant with the doings of the god of Abraham, Isaac, and Jacob: perhaps he had hoped the Hebrews might some day gain their freedom; if so, that hope had died out, and he was quietly passing his days in keeping the flocks of his father-in-law Jethro, in Midian.

Moses was approached through a voice in the burning bush, claiming to represent the god of Abraham, Isaac, and Jacob. This voice expressed the determination of that god to free his people

Israel, and desired the co-operation of Moses. Moses had no faith in the power of this god, and no hope of freeing his people. How was it possible for this god, alone, to cope with the enormous power of Egypt? He had no wish to become the leader of a forlorn-hope in any rash scheme for the deliverance of the Israelites.

We see Moses' want of faith in the power of this god, in the reluctance with which he accepted the position urged upon him, as the proposed leader of his people.

"Who am I" (he says), "that I should go unto Pharaoh, and that I should bring forth the children of Israel out of Egypt?" Being still further urged, he says, "When I shall come unto the children of Israel, and shall say unto them, The god of your fathers hath sent me unto you, and they shall say unto me, What is his name, what shall I say unto them?" When answered, he claims that "they will not believe me, nor hearken unto my voice." To meet his objections, he is given the power of miracles. He then makes the slowness and hesitation of his speech an excuse for not accepting; and, notwithstanding this god promises, "I will be with thy mouth, and teach thee what thou shalt say," he still hesitates, and seeks to get free from the proposed task. He beseeches the god to send some one else: "O my Lord, send,

I pray thee, by the hand of him whom thou wilt send." This unwillingness provokes the anger of the god; "and the anger of the Lord was kindled against Moses." His objection is met by appointing his brother Aaron as his spokesman, and declaring that to both his brother and to Pharaoh he (Moses) shall be as a god.

It was not, as has been said, the meekness of Moses that led him to refuse the office proposed. The objections come from a man fearing for himself, and doubting the power and ability of the god who desired his services, to carry out what he proposes; and who is consequently indisposed to take the prominent part insisted upon. He seeks in every way, by every subterfuge, to escape the task sought to be laid upon him; and it is not until he is driven from all his excuses, his faith strengthened by the power of performing miracles which is bestowed upon him, and by the promise of personal protection by reason of the belief that he is a god, which is to be planted in the mind of Pharaoh, that he accepts the position thus persistently urged upon him.

Moses was aware of the vast power of Egypt, and, like all others, supposed that power was obtained and retained by means of the good-will of their gods. They received enormous gifts and offerings; sacrifice and incense arose before them day and night; and in return they blessed Egypt with happiness, prosperity, and power: and Moses felt it to be a dangerous thing to proceed against such a power. He is led on by degrees; his first effort is against the weakest of the Egyptian gods. His success leads to more confidence in the power of Jehovah, until at last he has measured his power single-handed with them all. This confidence is shared by the Israelites, who at first, watching anxiously his movements, are encouraged, and finally are filled with joy and confidence.

The Deity further reveals himself to Moses by name as Jehovah: "the existing one." By my name Jehovah (he says) was I *not* known unto Abraham, Isaac, and Jacob.

As in former times the Deity revealed himself to Abraham as a household god, meeting the expectations and belief of those times; so now he takes a higher position, and proposes to make himself the tutelary or guardian god of a nation that he will form out of these Israelites. He will measure his strength with the gods of Egypt; will bring the Israelites out of bondage, and make them a nation. If he does this, they shall as a nation make choice of him as their guardian, tutelary, or national god; they shall be loyal to him, and serve and worship him alone. It is upon this platform that he proceeds against the gods of Egypt. The Israelites believed in the gods of Egypt, in their strength and power; and the Deity meets them in that belief, and uses it for his own purposes.

The bargain accords with the ideas of the Israelites; it is in unison with their desires, and with the belief ot the times. It is the proposition of a god without a people, desirous of becoming the protecting or tutelary god of a nation, instead of being the god of individuals or of a family. His proposition is, that he will prove his power; and if successful, he is to be their god. As the god of a nation, sacrifices would be offered daily; which, according to the belief of the times, was all that was desired by the gods. If he succeeds in his undertaking, they will gladly choose so powerful a god, as their national god, and will rejoice to be adopted by him.

This bargain or agreement is expressed by the Deity, as Jehovah, to Moses, as follows: —

"Now shalt thou see what I will do to Pharaoh, for with a strong hand shall he let them go, and with a strong hand shall he drive them out of his land. . . . Say unto the children of Israel, I am the Lord, and I will bring you out from under the burdens of the Egyptians, and I will rid you out of their bondage; and I will redeem you with a stretched-out arm, and with great judgments; and I will take you to me for a people, and I will be to you a God, and ye shall know that I am your God, which bringeth you out from under the burden of the Egyptians; and I will bring you in unto the land concerning the which I did swear to give it to Abraham, to Isaac, and to Jacob, and I will give it to you for an heritage; I am the Lord." This is the proposition of Jehovah to this people.

Here were two or three millions of bond men and women, a people robbed of all manliness by long years of servitude; slaves, ignorant and superstitious, desiring only creature comforts, satisfied with their servitude if only well fed; worshippers, if at all, of the gods of Egypt. These people, so debased, were under subjection to the most enlightened and powerful nation existing; at that time in the height of their power and glory; their country the seat of learning, arts, and civilization, and their gods the most powerful of any nation; with immense armies, and all the resources necessary for protection or offence; a nation whose interest it was to keep these people in bondage. How could Jehovah, alone and unaided, accomplish the work he proposed? How could he break the chains of the Israelites, and set them free, — one god against a dozen?

The effect of the first visit of Moses to Pharaoh was to increase the tasks of the Israelites, and they were angry at his interference. What could give them faith sufficient to take the first step for their own deliverance?

Moses was the mouthpiece, the representative, of Jehovah, — his agent. He must prove to them that Jehovah not only had the will, but also the power, to deliver them. He must bring them out of their bondage boldly, with force and might, and the exhibition of great strength. Not only must this be done without their help, but even in opposition to their fears; he must do it in such a manner as to win their confidence, and give them faith in the ability of Jehovah when exerted in contest with the gods of Egypt. These gods must be put to shame, their power mocked and brought to naught. This could only be done by the direct agency of Jehovah, exerted through Moses, in such stupendous and extraordinary exhibitions as should be seen and acknowledged of all; even the weakest and most timid of the Israelites must be able to boast of the triumphs of his god.

On the other side, how could Moses bring the Israelites out of bondage to the Egyptians, without their consent? and how would it be possible to obtain that consent?

There was no way to do this except by the use of the miraculous power placed in his hands by Jehovah for that purpose. The confidence and faith of the Egyptians in the power of their gods must be broken down and destroyed; and they must be made to realize that both their gods and themselves were wholly powerless before Jehovah, the mighty god of the Hebrews; that their lives were in his hands and at his mercy.

We see that the use of extraordinary and miraculous powers was necessary, on the one side, to inspire confidence in Jehovah; on the other, to arouse fear and dread of that being, by proving that he was not only more powerful than all the gods of Egypt, but that all attempts to withstand him would meet with disaster, defeat, and death.

The series of events, commonly called the plagues of Egypt, were direct and systematic attacks on the various gods worshipped by the Egyptians. As each in turn was shown to be powerless to prevent the plague or curse brought upon them, the faith of the Israelites in the gods of Egypt was weakened, and their confidence in Jehovah strengthened; until from the bloody water, the lice and frogs, to the fire and hail, the thick darkness, and the death of the first-born, all the Egyptian gods, one after another, had been defied, and found powerless to protect either themselves or their worshippers.

The Deity used this miraculous power for his own purposes. By its means he not only strengthened the faith of the Israelites, but, in the various occasions in which it was used, the name of Jehovah was spread abroad, his power became known, and a fear of him existed in other nations.

Here was a nation of bondmen. Fear was the only means of teaching, or keeping in subjection, these millions of rude, uneducated human beings, but little above the animals; slaves to their appetites and passions; a huge, unwieldy mob of ignorant, lawless, headstrong men, women, and children, suddenly relieved from bondage of body and soul, left now at liberty to work their own sweet wills without let or hinderance; with only one man to say them nay, and he self-elected to the position of leader, with no standing army to enforce his behests, no system of laws or punishments to keep them in subjection, and, if there had been, with no civil power to enforce those punishments. How could this one man keep these hosts in subjection? By his own power alone, it was impossible. It was necessary at the start, and would be necessary throughout, for Jehovah himself so to enforce obedience to Moses and his requirements, that they should know and feel that punishment would inevitably follow transgression; and that it would be quick, stern, and unrelenting.

Notwithstanding the manifold and great miracles performed in relieving them from bondage, we see how weak and craven these Israelites were. The first apparent difficulty led them to fear the approach of Pharaoh and his hosts, and to question and distrust the power that had so far aided them; but the miracle of the passage of the Red Sea, and the destruction of the chariots, horsemen, and army of Pharaoh, again restored confidence in Jehovah.

Having brought this people out of bondage, supplied them with water at Horeb, overcome the Amalekites, and brought them to a place of peace and safety, the next thing to be done was to establish the authority and government of Jehovah as their god, and of Moses as his servant, and the medium through whom his will should be expressed.

It is said of the American Indian, that when the whites first settled the country they found the native inhabitants believed in the Great Spirit, and in a place of reward for the good Indian hereafter in the happy hunting-grounds. This belief is far in advance of the religious ideas of the Israelites at the time of Moses. They did not believe in Jehovah as a spiritual god, but as a god in form like unto a man, and very much like the gods of other nations, only more powerful. They had no belief in, or thought of, any other life than the present. Moses, if he had any higher belief (which is doubtful), taught it not. His whole system of government, of reward and punishment, is confined to this world. Indeed, the Israelites were too low, debased, and ignorant to understand any religion, or any system of government, that did not apply itself to the gratification of their animal nature, to their creature comforts and pleasures, and worldly happiness, on the one hand; or to their fear of want, sickness, pain, and discomfort, on the other. Deity meets them on the par of their knowledge, on their own plane of thought; and gradually, in after-years, enlightens them, until the time finally comes when the full revelation of himself in Christ can be understood and appreciated. But now the Israelites must be kept in subjection by fear.

Moses was required by Jehovah to call the children of Israel together. He rehearses to them the action of Jehovah in bringing them out of bondage, and makes to them this proposition from Jehovah as a contract or covenant: " Now therefore, if you will obey my voice indeed, and keep my covenant, then you shall be a peculiar treasure unto me above all people (for all the earth is mine), and ye shall be unto me a kingdom of priests, and an holy nation."

"Then all the people answered with one voice, and said: All the words which the Lord hath said, will we do."

As the result of this agreement, a covenant was formed. "And Moses wrote all the words of the Lord. . . . And Moses took the book of the covenant, and read in the audience of the people; and they said, All that the Lord hath said will we do, and be obedient."

"And Moses took the blood, and sprinkled it on the people, and said, Behold the blood of the covenant which the Lord hath made with you concerning all these words."

By this contract, thus ratified and sealed, Jehovah agreed that they should be to him a peculiar people, a kingdom of priests, and a holy nation. For the position thus given, and the protection and care promised, the Israelites agreed to obey him, and to faithfully keep the contract or covenant on their part.

The consent of the Israelites having been given, Moses proceeded to proclaim a system of government suitable for the people over whom he had been called to rule. Having no earthly power to enforce these precepts, or uphold his authority, his position must be upheld by Jehovah as against all others. Moses being his agent, his mouthpiece, all laws emanating from him are the laws of Jehovah, and must be so enforced.

Jehovah having been chosen by them as their god, no swerving from their allegiance to him was allowed. All other nations gave the credit of their successes to their god or gods: so must the Hebrews. They must offer sacrifices to no other god: such an offering would be disloyalty, and must be punished. He was to be approached with awe and reverence. They must fear him.

The priesthood were taught caution by the death of Aaron's sons, who offered strange fire before the altar. Murmuring against God was punished by the plague caused by eating quails; rebellion against Moses, by the leprosy of Miriam, and the destruction of Korah, Dathan, and Abiram, and their adherents. In these and other cases the punishment was direct and severe; and the Israelites were finally brought into obedience to Moses, and to a partial observance of their covenant with Jehovah.

In accomplishing these objects, extraordinary exhibitions of the power of Jehovah were manifested, not only in the exceptional cases of the violent and quick destruction of thousands of the Israelites, but in the daily miracles, which, from their continuance, must have seemed to the

Israelites as the due course of nature, — the pillar of cloud and of fire, the daily manna, and its miracle of remaining over the sabbath.

The Israelites had deliberately chosen Jehovah as their god, and accepted the obligations of their contract with him. He in turn had agreed to fulfil the obligations imposed on him as tutelary god of the nation.

These agreements are matter of record; and, that there may be no mistake on the part of the people, Moses wrote these obligations in a book, which was kept in the ark, — a vessel of safety or deposit; the ark of the covenant. In it were written the rewards, or blessings, which the nation should receive or obtain by compliance with the requirements of the law; and also the punishments, or cursings, which disobedience would entail or bring upon the nation. This "book of the law" we have in all its essential parts, as originally written by Moses.

This was but the commencement of forty years of teaching and care. During these years, the original covenant was enlarged and accepted by the Israelites with due solemnities.

Jehovah was represented, in the pillar of cloud and fire, daily before them; yet we see how difficult it was, to keep them subject to the teachings and laws of Moses. During these forty years, the people were born again, free men, knowing no master but Jehovah, and no service but his. With the exception of the leaders, none of them had known slavery, nor had they been worshippers of the gods of Egypt. Yet Moses, ere he departed, foretold their backsliding, their serving of other gods, and the punishments that would follow.

Later, they are taught by priests and holy men, warned by prophets, rewarded when they served Jehovah, punished when they turned from him and served other gods. And yet, what a history it is! a history of failures to the end.

Under the guidance of Joshua, the Hebrews entered the promised land, a people, large in numbers, without civilization, a horde of savages. Without experience in war, poorly armed, and with but slight means of attack, they overcame the nations possessing the soil, and obtained possession of the land promised to their fathers, Abraham, Isaac, and Jacob.

The Canaanites were advanced in civilization, having a knowledge of many of the arts, living in cities with paved streets, lined with houses of stone, and surrounded with stone walls.[1] This people were also advanced in wickedness and sin, as well as in civilization. They worshipped Baal,

---

[1] Many of these cities still exist; the houses, in some instances, remain to-day as perfect as when built, but uninhabited.

Ashtoreth, Moloch, and other gods. Human sacrifice was common; they frequently offered their own children on the altar, for personal favors, or length of life. The worship of Ashtoreth or Venus was accompanied by orgies the most infamous and foul.

These nations would be a snare to the Israelites. They were too debased, too polluted, to be allowed to live; and Jehovah determined to eradicate them, not by flood or earthquake or fire, but by war. These licentious and debased nations should be blotted out of existence.

Even in these punishments, Jehovah meets man on the plane of his belief and practice. A religion of mercy could not have been understood by the Hebrews. The punishments or cursings of their own "law of the Lord" threatened the same consequences that they were required to deal out to the Canaanites. Earthly reward was the incentive to virtue, and earthly punishment was the preventive of vice; and these were the only ones that would have had the slightest effect on them.

We know how they failed in carrying out these requirements of Jehovah, that were necessary for their own protection, and the result foretold took place. The Israelites were contaminated. They neglected the worship of Jehovah, and served the

gods of the Canaanites, until at times they appear
to have been worse, if possible, than the Canaanites
themselves. In punishment for their sins, they
became tributary to, and were ruled over by, the
Canaanitish nations. Occasionally, when their
sufferings had led them to turn to Jehovah for
help, a hero would arise, and, in the strength of
his faith in the god of his people, would release
them from bondage. When they became a nation,
the same results followed. When they obeyed and
worshipped Jehovah, peace, prosperity, and plenty
reigned in the land. If they departed from their
faith, and worshipped and served other gods, they
were punished by war, famine, disease, or some
other curse of the law.

But God's purposes were fulfilled as well in the
disobedience of the Hebrews, as in their obedience. Through their disobedience they were
scattered abroad among all nations; and disaster,
bringing them back to their service and faith in
Jehovah, led to a knowledge of the God of the
Hebrews by other nations; and thus each of these
occurrences was a step in advance in the plans of
the Deity, and the Hebrews were used as instruments of his will, even in their wilfulness and sin.

During their existence as a nation, many
prophets and wise men appeared among them,
exhorting them to obedience and loyalty to

Jehovah, and threatening them with disaster for non-obedience. These constantly magnified the power of Jehovah, gradually enlarged the spiritual nature of his requirements, and endeavored to lead the Hebrews to a purer and higher faith. They also prophesied against many of the nations with whom the Hebrews came in contact. The fulfilment of these predictions strengthened the faith of the Hebrews in the accomplishment of those particularly affecting themselves; they were also intended, doubtless, to have the same effect on other nations who should see their completion. The faith of the Jews was intensified, and their religious views enlarged, by these means. Each advance was a step toward the object pursued by the Deity in gradually bringing the minds of the civilized races of the earth to the point at which they would be ready to receive the spiritual teachings of his evangel.

There are three distinct periods of existence for man on this earth, — the animal, the intellectual, and the spiritual. In the five thousand years of the Aryas' occupation of the Garden of Eden, they advanced by slow steps from the animal to the intellectual, and finally at the time of Adam were fully enjoying the spiritual period.

The Hebrew people, when they became the wards of Jehovah, had just emerged from the animal, and were but entering the intellectual period; the spiritual was unseen and unknown to them.

This ignorant and superstitious race required entirely different methods of instruction from those adapted to the Aryas. Like some scientific men of the present day, *they* required God to be present to their senses; they must be able to see, taste, smell, hear, and feel him. The Deity met these requirements by exhibitions of his presence in the pillar of cloud and fire, and in the shechinah, or luminous presence on the ark; by cleaving the Red Sea; by the thunders of Horeb and Sinai; by the daily supply of manna; by the destruction of the walls of Jericho, and by many other direct deviations from the usually observed action of his natural laws.

In the history of the Hebrews from their exode to their captivity in Babylon, as written by Nehemiah, we can trace the continual and exact fulfilment, on the part of Jehovah, of the contract entered into by him with the Hebrew race.

It is evident that the Hebrews did not see, in the destruction of Jerusalem and the temple, a final ending and annulling of their contract, — that they had been tried, and found wanting.

There were prophecies made to Abraham and to Moses as yet unfulfilled. The prophets had given them visions of a great and glorious king, who should come in the might and power of Jehovah, and sit upon the throne of David as the ruler of the world; and they commenced the establishment of a new kingdom, the building of a new city, and the erection of a new temple, in the full belief that they were the old ones revived, and that their contract with Jehovah was still in force.

During their seventy years' captivity, the Jews were sifted; great numbers returned to the original faith of their forefather Abraham, previous to his departure from Ur. Of the large number who were carried into captivity, and their descendants, the most earnest of them alone returned to rebuild Jerusalem. From that time there was no more backsliding; they became true worshippers of Jehovah, and believers in the contract made with him by their fathers.

III.

THE JEWS.

CYRUS TO THE CHRIST.

By permission of Cyrus, B.C. 536, about fifty thousand Chaldæan Jews, descendants of the Hebrews that had been carried into captivity, returned to rebuild and rehabilitate Jerusalem.

"By the rivers of Babylon we sat down and wept," appears to have been more a poetical figure of speech than the truth. Jeremiah had told them that their captivity would be long, and advised them, "Build ye houses, and dwell in them; plant gardens, and eat the fruit of them." They took kindly to this advice, became willing colonists and contented subjects. This is shown in the fact, that of all the millions of Judah and Israel that had been carried into captivity during the previous two hundred years, and their descendants, so small a percentage had sufficient interest in the country and religion of their fathers to return to Jerusalem, and join in re-inhabiting the land.

One hundred years before the downfall of Jerusalem, the residue of Israel had been carried into captivity by the Assyrians. Of the inhabitants of Judah, two hundred thousand were carried away captive by Sennacherib, B. C. 702. Esarhaddon, about B.C. 670, carried away great numbers; and in the taking of Jerusalem, B.C. 606, and the final demolishing of the walls and burning of the city, B.C. 582, probably a million or more men, women, and children were carried into captivity.

Their natural growth during seventy years of peace must have largely increased their original numbers. Under these circumstances, the few (only one or two per cent of the whole number) that availed themselves of the opportunity offered to return to the country of their fathers, the land of promise, is evidence of the lightness of their bonds, of the liberty enjoyed by them in Babylonia and Persia, and of the fact that the Jewish religion had lost its hold on vast numbers of them.

In fact, the Hebrews, never tenacious in their religious beliefs, had in their captivity to a great degree adopted the religion of the Babylonians. It was the original religion of their father Abram; and they easily transferred their allegiance from the defeated god, Jehovah, to the gods of Babylonia. Others, who still retained the religion of their fathers, were bound to the country of their captivity by local attachments, or by ties of blood or interest. With the usual thrift of their nation, many had become merchants, and waxed rich in this centre of the world's wealth and commerce; and, with the greater part, the memories and traditions of their fatherland had died out, and the plenty and luxuriance of their present home outweighed the promise of the old. The Book of Daniel gives us some knowledge of their political position; and the Book of Esther shows that later, in the days of the Persian King Artaxerxes, — the biblical Ahasuerus, — the Jews enjoyed exceptional position and power, one of the daughters of the race being the favorite queen of that monarch.

The new and struggling nationality of the Jews at Jerusalem received but little help from Persia. Intercourse between the Jews at Jerusalem and those in Persia was comparatively infrequent. For a long time Jerusalem, with its out-lying towns, was dependent on itself for life, growth, and support. This growth was at first very slow, and surrounded with difficulties, owing to the repeated interruptions and the enmity of the Samaritans, aided by the Ammonites, Moabites, and others.

Seventy-nine years after the return to Jerusalem, they were still in a chaotic state; and, B.C. 457, Artaxerxes sent Ezra with some fifteen hundred emigrants to Jerusalem, with directions to aid and encourage the Jews in restoring and rebuilding the walls, and re-peopling the city. Ezra introduced some reforms, and corrected some irregularities and abuses; but, being a quiet and studious man, he added but little to the religious welfare of the people.

Eleven years later, B.C. 445, Nehemiah was sent from Persia with the king's commission as governor, taking with him a thousand families.

Aroused by him to new exertions, the Jews in the short space of two months rebuilt the city wall, working with weapons at hand, ready at a moment's notice to repel an attack from the surrounding foes. The reforms begun by Ezra were sustained by the power of Nehemiah. Gifts flowed into the treasury of the temple, and the deserted streets of Jerusalem were repeopled from the surrounding country.

Nehemiah translated the "book of the law" from the Hebrew, and wrote the history of its origin, and the results to the nation, in the Aramaic tongue, the language then used by the Jews, and assisted greatly in placing the new nation on a permanent material and religious basis. With the exception of a few brief visits to Persia, Nehemiah administered the government at Jerusalem for forty years.[1] His work and influ-

---

[1] Authorities vary with regard to the length of Nehemiah's term of office. The work done by him, and the stability given to the new nationality, would indicate a much longer time than twelve years.

ence gave permanent shape and form to the new nationality.

For two hundred years Palestine was a province of and dependent on Persia for protection, peace, and prosperity.

Under Persian influence the Jews imbibed some of the Persian habits of thought and belief. The Zoroastrian doctrine of one god, a spirit and invisible, maker and ruler of the universe, had in the course of centuries been changed. The original monotheism had became a dualism; a god of evil had been added, who was believed to be the especial foe of the Deity. These antagonistic forces of good and evil were supposed to be in continual conflict, and each of these powers had allied to them, and under their control, beings of inferior positions, and of various degrees of station and influence, such as angels, archangels, and powers of light on one side, and demons, devils, and powers of darkness on the other. The Persians also believed in immortality and in a state of future reward and punishment.

The religion of the Jews, as taught by Moses, became enlarged in some respects by these influences. The national god of the Jews, instead of being simply a local god, warring with other deities on a par of equality, was gradually endowed by them with the Persian idea of a spiritual god, maker and ruler of heaven and earth, before whom all other gods were but as dust in the balance. Moses, in his religious system, had no god of evil. Now, for the first time, the Jews recognize a power antagonistic to God, and teach hesitatingly a future life of reward and punishment for deeds done in the body.

In the absence of nobility, the priestly class had obtained an ascendancy. The book of the law was regarded with superstitious reverence, as containing the record of their contract with Jehovah; and its laws became the laws of the land. The Messianic predictions began to have effect; and slowly there grew up among the people the idea of a great conqueror before whom all nations should bow the knee, and whose dominion should be everlasting.

In the overthrow of Persia, B. C. 331, Palestine became tributary to Alexander the Great. B. C. 320, Ptolemy, King of Egypt, became their ruler; and they continued under the Grecian yoke for about one hundred and fifty years, until the independence achieved by the Maccabees about B. C. 168. They continued independent until conquered by Pompey, B. C. 63, and were subject to Rome until the destruction of Jerusalem, A. D. 70.

In the Hebrew scriptures we see the Deity form a rude, uncultivated horde into a nation. We see him teach that nation by wise men and prophets, by prosperity and adversity, all the incidents of which they have recorded. We see him using this nation through all their sin and wandering, in happiness and misery, in plenty and want, in freedom and captivity, to advance his purpose. We see the name and power of Jehovah spread abroad among the nations, and the expected Messiah known to all.

The evidence of all this is stronger, because unintentional. These records were kept by the Hebrews for the purpose of showing the original compacts, and their literal fulfilment on the part of Jehovah. The prophets foretold the coming of a Messiah who should wield extraordinary power, through whom the original promise made to Abraham, that "In thy seed shall all the nations of the earth be blessed," should be fulfilled. To him were given names and titles of power and majesty. His glory was magnified, and his coming reign was extolled in such glowing language, that the Hebrews, whose thoughts centred on this world, finally looked upon the coming Messiah as a king who should rule over the whole earth, and the Jewish nation by his means should become the ruling power in the world.

Under this belief, the Hebrews guarded with care all the evidences and records of the contract made by Jehovah with their nation; forgetting that these very records condemned them, as having repeatedly broken their contract, and made it null and void.

Believing, that as he had kept faith with them of old, had many times forgiven their backsliding, and had fulfilled all the obligations of the contract so far, he would continue to do so, they kept these records with great care and faithfulness.

At the time of Christ, the Aryan race, which four or five thousand years before had been forced from civilization, and scattered to the ends of the earth, had again become rulers of Western Asia, Egypt, and Europe, and the leaders in civilization.

Five hundred years before this period, the first advance had been made by the Persian Aryas, who conquered Western Asia and Egypt. Two hundred years later, the Grecian Aryas ruled the same countries and Southern Europe. And now for sixty years the Roman Aryas had ruled the civilized world.

When, by permission of Cyrus, a portion of the Jews returned to Jerusalem, by far the greater number remained in Babylonia. At a later period the Jewish colonies in Egypt rivalled in numbers the Babylonian colonies, each far outnumbering the Jews in Palestine. At Alexandria in Egypt two-fifths of the population were Jews. They had a temple at On, or Heliopolis, and a large and beautiful synagogue in Alexandria, and enjoyed the privilege of worshipping Jehovah without hinderance.

Professor Allen, in his "Hebrew Men and Times," says, "Coming in direct contact with Grecian learning and philosophy, the Jews in Egypt gradually embodied with their own belief many Grecian ideas; and as we approach the Christian era, we find in their writings evidences of new and enlarged views. Additions were made to the Talmud, mysticisms and speculations were rife; the imagery of the Greeks had become partially incorporated in the Jewish faith and appeared in their writings."

Philo, an Alexandrian Jew of a priestly family, in the latter part of the first century B.C., was a voluminous writer. He says, "None but a fool would think the world was made in six days, or in any given period of time; since it is the Divine nature to act always, and creation is eternal." The record of creation, narratives of Adam and Eve, Cain and Abel, Abraham, Isaac, and Jacob, Abraham's visit to Egypt, and offering up Isaac, he claims are all allegories.

The Wisdom of Solomon is supposed to have been written by a Grecian Jew at about or after the time of Christ, and shows the advance in

Jewish thought at that time. "God," it says, "is the lover of souls. . . . His spirit filleth the world. . . . God created man to be immortal, and made him to be an image of his own eternity." "The souls of the righteous are in the hand of God, and there shall no torment touch them; for though they be punished in the sight of men, yet is their hope full of immortality."

These enlarged views were most prevalent among the Egyptian Jews. We have no evidence that they had permeated to any great extent the Jews of Palestine. While the Egyptian Jews, under a government tolerating all religions, had become cosmopolitan, the various troubles in Palestine — the chronic state of rebellion in which the inhabitants indulged, their frequent uprisings, their sullen obedience, and revengeful utterances — caused the Roman government to use the strong arm of military power in repressing the turbulent expressions and acts of the populace. This unsettled state of affairs, so different from the freedom of Egypt, prevented migration from thence; and the enlightened views of the Jews of Alexandria had but little effect in the mother country, and were certainly unknown to the common people, whose ideas bore more of the stamp of Persian influence than of Greek culture and habit of thought.

While, in the five hundred years of exile during which the Jews had been scattered over the whole civilized world, their views in general had been enlarged, in Palestine they had added but little to the crude and primitive religion of Moses. Larger and grander ideas of Jehovah had been imbibed; he was their *one* god; they believed him to be stronger and more powerful than all the gods of the nations; they feared and were proud of him: in all else, they remained an ignorant, bigoted, and self-righteous people.

They generally believed Jehovah to be the creator and sustainer of the universe: yet he still remained, as they thought, the god of their nation, and held them in particular regard; they were his chosen people; he had made a compact with their fathers which they believed to be still in force, and they were impatiently awaiting the appearance of that Messiah, who, as his anointed and chosen son and representative, should restore Israel to more than the former glory under David and Solomon.

These ideas of the future greatness of their race, and the nearness of the time, led them to be arrogant and haughty. They looked with contempt on all the nations of the earth; intercourse with them was confined to the necessities of the occasion, and to eat with them was to become unclean.

Some of the more enlightened of the Jews, notably the Pharisees, believed in a future life, and in a future state of reward and punishment. This belief was held with fear and trembling. Moses taught it not. They had no certainty; and in promulgating the doctrine, they did so with such reservations as to lead the common people afterward to contrast the hesitancy of their teachings with the directness and certainty of the doctrines of the Christ, and to say of him, that he "spoke like one having authority, and not as the scribes."

The Jews of Jerusalem nursed their pride and their feelings of revenge, by the hope and belief that the time was at hand when their promised Christ should appear, and establish the new kingdom or rule of heaven.

The imagery of Isaiah and other prophets had been magnified into a glorious picture of a Messiah who should suddenly appear in the temple in great glory, clothed in the power and majesty of Jehovah, wielding the sceptre of dominion, — a prophet like unto Moses, with more than his power of miracle; a son of God empowered from on high with the execution of those deeds and acts which should place Judah on a pinnacle of glory, the ruling power of the whole world; a Messiah as king, who was to put all enemies under his feet, and rule forever; all people, nations, and languages should serve him; his kingdom was to be an everlasting kingdom, and his rule without end; he was to be of the line of David, a king by divine right, and anointed by Jehovah, one whose sway was to be indisputable, irresistible, and universal.

The time for his appearance was already at hand, as they believed; and each day they awaited with painful expectation his coming. But the days passed, time went on, and no Messiah made his appearance. They had waited until they had become heart-sick, and they hoped against hope, for the fulfilment of their Messianic dreams.

Jehovah's system of rewards and punishments had been confined to this world; it was the only system that would have effect on the minds of the Hebrews, or be a sufficient incentive for them to follow the requirements of the law.

This habit of thought led the Jews of this period to expect in the promised Messiah a temporal prince, who by miraculous means should overcome all resistance, and become the ruler of the world.

While *we* can see that all the prophecies are fulfilled in Christ's spiritual kingdom and power, and to a greater extent than would have been possible in any worldly sway, yet we can also see how natural to the Jew was the literal understanding of the prophetic utterances, and the strong belief that they would be fulfilled in the Christ.

Previous to the destruction of Jerusalem, large numbers of the Hebrews had fled to Egypt. Here they increased in numbers, and became an important part of the population. Also, great numbers of those carried into Babylon remained there, under the Persian sway; they filled many positions of trust and honor, and became the merchants and traders of the country.

From these two centres of civilization, trade and commerce carried the Hebrew to all parts of the civilized world, and their faith became known in all countries.

The character of Jehovah as displayed in their history was infinitely superior to that of any of the heathen deities; and in the superior power and position that had become associated with his name, the thoughtful of other nations recognized a god whom they could reverence and worship.

Thus, in the hands of the Deity, the Hebrew nation had become an instrument through whom he was known as the powerful Jehovah, and the way had been prepared for the great revelation through the Christ.

ANNO DOMINI.

About this time a child was born in the little town of Bethlehem near Jerusalem, of whom some wonderful stories were told by a few persons who had become cognizant of the events; but the interest excited at the time soon passed away, and, had it not been for other incidents happening at a later period in the life of the child, they would have been forgotten and lost.

The father of the child was named Joseph, a carpenter by trade; the mother's name was Mary; she is supposed to have been Joseph's second wife. Both were of the line of David. They had left Nazareth, their native city, and journeyed to Bethlehem to be enrolled for the purpose of taxation by the Roman Government.[1]

While in this place a son was born. The khan or inn being full, they had been obliged to occupy a portion of the building usually given over to cattle; and for want of better accommodation the child was cradled in a manger, or crib, from which the cattle generally ate their food.

In the early morning, soon after the birth of the child, some shepherds appeared, and related a strange tale of angels who had appeared to them while they were watching their sheep, one of whom, addressing them, had proclaimed the joyful tidings that the long-expected Messiah had that day been born, and directed them how to find the child; and then a multitude of the heavenly host united in songs of praise to God, who had remem-

[1] Professor Allen of Harvard University places the date of this event A.D. 7.

bered his promise, and had sent a Saviour to his people. The shepherds, following the directions given by the angel, found this child, and then paid homage to him who they had been informed was "the Saviour, Christ the Lord."

The child, having been presented in the temple on the eighth day, was named Jesus. He was recognized by Simeon, a just and devout Jew, as the "Lord's Christ" or Anointed; and also by Anna, a prophetess, who gave thanks to God, and "spoke of him to all them that looked for redemption in Jerusalem."

Several months afterward, the inhabitants of Jerusalem were surprised by the visit of wise men from the East (probably Jews from Babylonia and Persia), inquiring for the king of the Jews; and as their inquiries had especial reference to the Messiah, as the king whose birth they proclaimed, and whom they desired to find, they were directed by the priests to Bethlehem, as the town in which it had been foretold he would be born.

These wise men — guided by a star which they called his star — were conducted to the residence of Joseph and Mary; there they paid obeisance to the child as to a king, and presented him with such gifts and offerings as were usually given to a child born heir to a kingdom; and from thence they departed homeward. Shortly after, the parents and child visited Egypt, apparently staying several years, and then returned to their former home, Nazareth.

At this time, when he was perhaps five or six years old, it is recorded of the child, that "he grew, and waxed strong in spirit, filled with wisdom, and the grace of God was upon him." This is the noble and exceptional character given of him as a child.

When Jesus was twelve years old, he visited Jerusalem with his parents, and showed much interest in and intelligence about Jewish history and religion. His precocity of intellect, and maturity of thought, astonished the wise men and teachers at the temple; and the record we have of him about this time is, that "he increased in wisdom and in stature, and in favor with God and man."

We have no further knowledge of Jesus until he was "about thirty years of age," A.D. 37.

Several months previous to this time, a man named John had suddenly appeared in the desert places of Judæa, dressed in the garb of a prophet, proclaiming the kingdom of heaven, or the rule or government of heaven, to be at hand. This was the long-looked-for and expected announcement for which the Jews were waiting. The coming of the Christ the Anointed of God, and the establishment of his kingdom, they desired and longed for. They were tired of waiting for it, and had almost given up hope; but here was a messenger giving them new life. The kingdom of heaven was at hand. The government of the whole world was about to be placed in the hands of the Jews. The glorious king through whose power (received directly from Jehovah) they were to conquer their enemies was soon to come; and with awakened expectation they went out from Jerusalem and the country round about, to see this new prophet, and hear from his own lips the glad tidings he announced.

They found this man proclaiming the coming of the long-promised Messiah, at the same time, however, calling on them to turn from their sins, to repent, and become better men; that all injustice should be done away with, that they must deal honestly, aid each other, and prepare for the coming of the Christ by cleansing themselves from their sins. It was not enough for them to be Abraham's children: he who was coming would search the heart; only those who should bring forth the fruits of righteousness would be received into the new kingdom. As an acknowledgment that they accepted these terms, he required them to be baptized.

These strange doctrines surprised and puzzled them. The scribes and Pharisees more especially were confounded. They were unable to see why these doctrines should be preached and insisted upon as preparatory to the coming of a conqueror and king, — of a man who should by force of arms conquer the world. The excitement caused by this extraordinary preaching was great, and the fame of the new prophet spread over the whole of Palestine. Large numbers acknowledged their belief in him, and were baptized in public acknowledgment of their faith.

Among others who came to hear the new prophet was Jesus. He was in the flush of manhood, perfect in form and feature, and full of intellectual and moral vigor. He was known among his friends and countrymen as a dutiful and industrious son, a loving friend and neighbor, having a forgiving disposition, a compassionate spirit, an unblemished reputation, and as fulfilling all the duties of his position with energy and rectitude.

Known to John as a man of pure mind and upright life and conversation, the application of Jesus to receive the baptism of repentance at his hands seemed to him inappropriate. His first impulse was to refuse, to disclaim for himself the implication of superior holiness: it would be more in accordance with his feelings, himself to receive baptism from the hands of Jesus. Jesus answered that he believed in the doctrines taught by John, and that it was proper that he should show his belief by receiving the same rite given to others. To this reasoning John assented, and baptized him.

On emerging from the water, an extraordinary scene occurred: an appearance like unto a dove descended from heaven, and alighted on Jesus; at the same time a voice was heard declaring, "This is my well-beloved Son, in him I am well pleased."

JESUS THE CHRIST.

Previous to his birth, Mary, the mother of Jesus, had been informed that her son was to be the Christ. The tidings of the shepherds, the acknowledgments of Simeon and Anna, the visit and offerings of the magi, all had confirmed the statement, and strengthened the belief in her heart. Yet what did she see? Her child growing up to youth, to manhood, and on to thirty years of age or more, without one sign that these promises were to be fulfilled. Where were the evidences that these statements were true? Where were the glory and the splendor that were to be his? Where was the throne of his father David, which Jehovah was to give him? where the power that was to be bestowed upon him?

Mary was of a devout and affectionate disposition, reticent in all matters concerning herself and her son, "pondering them in her heart." It cannot be supposed, however, that she had never informed her child of the circumstances of his birth, and of the prophecies concerning him, both those in the Hebrew Scriptures, and those personal to herself. We may well believe that even long previous to his visit to Jerusalem at twelve years of age, he had received and pondered over this information, and had studied with enthusiasm the many prophecies of the power, grandeur, and universal rule of the coming Messiah whom he believed to be himself. With these feelings overpowering his mind, he takes this first opportunity to question the doctors relative to the prophecies respecting the Christ, which were in many respects apparently contradictory in their character; and his searching inquiries and earnest reasoning may well have puzzled these wise men. This also gives a key to his meaning as he inquires, "Know ye not I must be about my Father's business?" must be preparing for the station I am to hold, the position I am to fill, as the Saviour and King of my country and of the world.

With the impatience of youth, we may suppose he was already preparing for the part he supposed he was to play in the great events of the future as a leader and king. Yet the record says,

"He was obedient unto" his parents. Even the dreams of future power did not prevent him from dutifully obeying them.

As time advances, we may see Jesus quietly awaiting the call to action. His youth passes, and manhood is reached, still with nothing to designate him as likely to take any active part in liberating his country from the Roman rule. Would not doubts suggest themselves to him? Was his mother not mistaken? Did she not dream? Was she in her right mind when she supposed she saw and heard the things of which she had informed him? How was he, a poor carpenter, supporting himself and mother by daily manual labor, — how was he to obtain followers? Who was he, that he should command armies? he, whose tastes were entirely opposed to bloodshed? How was he to govern a nation, much less the whole world?

While we may suppose thoughts kindred to these at times occupied his mind, at other times the conviction of the truth of his mother's statements would fill his heart; and, while awaiting any movement which in God's good time might take place, he fulfils the duties of the hour, and prepares himself for whatever revelation may be made.

We do not see him proud, vain-glorious, boastful, proclaiming abroad the position he was to hold. His mother and himself were both reticent, retiring; no one ever heard either of them speak of their hopes or expectations.

Do we not see in all this the fact that Jesus was "tempted in all points like as we are, yet without sin"? In all this watching and waiting, the hardest thing for an earnest man to do, was not the temptation strong to take the matter into his own hands, instead of awaiting the slow movement of events?

Thus he goes on: thirty years of age is reached, and still he has received no call to action. Finally he hears of the preaching of John: "The kingdom of heaven is at hand." The Messiah is about to appear! Can it be? He has received no intimation. Is he mistaken, after all? Are all his thoughts, his expectations, dreams? Is he doomed to utter disappointment? Must he put away his long-cherished hopes, and see the work accomplished by some one else?

With humility of heart, and humbled by his long self-delusion, he approaches and listens to the prophet.

He is glad that the Messiah is coming, although *he* is not the chosen one of God. He crucifies all his old and cherished feelings and desires, bows down in humble self-abasement, and in lowliness of spirit asks for the baptism of repentance at the hands of John.

Up to this time we find no evidence in the record that Jesus had any knowledge differing from that of other men. Being in the flesh, clothed upon by the animal, he partook of the same spiritual disadvantages belonging to us all. Spiritual beings, children of the most high God, we are enveloped in a garment of flesh which bounds our view; we know not whence we are, or whither we go. The material existence of the present is alone known to us; we see through the organ called the eye, as through the window of a prison-cell; our vision is confined, and we know nothing beyond, unless enlightened by the Spirit of God. He can give us the power to pierce through the earthly matter, and see the spiritual things around us.

As we observe the operations of God's Spirit in those to whom it was given, as related in the Hebrew Scriptures, we find it enlightened them in a certain direction and to a certain extent only. It was a special gift for certain specific purposes, and outside of those special objects the holders of the gift remained as before. Moses had the power of miracle placed in his hands, that he might fulfil the purposes of the Deity. The prophets were enlightened by the Holy Spirit in one direction, and generally in that only.

Up to this time, Jesus, as a child, boy, man, was a human being, tried and tempted even beyond the common lot of men, with all the loves, hopes, fears, and desires, the ills and sicknesses, of other men. The animal nature was as strong in him as in any other man, and needed the same control. He was living in this animal body, subject to all the imperfections of the flesh, as are all mankind. But now a new scene opens before him. He is startled, as are those about him, by the appearance and the voice accompanying it, in which he is commended as the well-beloved Son of God. This acknowledgment of the Deity answered the belief and expectation of the Jews, that the Christ should be the Son of Jehovah.

Stunned, amazed, he leaves the scene of his baptism; and driven by conflicting emotions, which crowd into and confuse his mind, he seeks the solitude of the desert, that he may there collect his scattered thoughts, and mature his plans for the future.

The few short passages which he has left us of the temptations in the wilderness give us the key to long and painful struggles before he had conquered, and deliberately chosen the path he afterward so unflinchingly trod.

A Jew, brought up and taught as a Jew, with all the Jewish hopes and longings, intensified in his own case because of his belief in himself and his destiny, he finds those hopes suddenly fulfilled.

He *is* the acknowledged and chosen Son of Jehovah, the predicted ruler of the world, the expected Messiah, the Saviour of his people.

All the ideas of his youth, the proud feeling of conscious strength and power, rush upon him. Now the hopes and desires of his countrymen will be realized. They shall indeed be relieved from their hated bonds to the Roman. The Roman rule shall be broken, and they shall be free; and, beyond that, his victorious legions, with the powerful aid which Jehovah has placed in his hands, shall subdue the whole world, and the prophecies be completed and fulfilled in him. All nations should bow down before him, and serve him; and he would be king and ruler over all. He would govern in righteousness; all wrongs should be righted, and he would give to the world peace. His sway would be universal and undisputed, and prosperity and happiness should abound in all the earth.

As these ideas shape themselves in his mind, others arise in conflict with them. Half-forgotten prophecies respecting Christ, his afflictions, his rejection, force themselves upon him; and as the turmoil of his thoughts subsides, and he grows more calm, other thoughts and ideas present themselves. They take a higher and grander position; he sees with more clearness the demands upon him. War is a great and serious evil. Bloodshed, murder, rapine, all the evils attending it, fill his heart with sorrow and aversion; he cannot be the means of filling the land with such horror. He must not tempt Jehovah to aid him in any such undertakings. Some other way must be found to establish the kingdom of heaven, the rule of Jehovah upon earth.

As he grows calmer, and proceeds to examine closer his relations to God and to his country, we may believe the Spirit of God enlightens him, and ideas before unknown are presented to him.

We see in one of the pictures in the temptations the desire to introduce himself to his countrymen by some startling miracle, like that of throwing himself from the pinnacle of the temple, thereby showing to all the fact of his miraculous power, and by so doing leading his countrymen to believe in him as the Messiah, the Christ of God. But this again is rejected, and gradually dawns on him the real character of his mission. He is a free agent. The power of miracle is in his hands, to use it as he sees fit. He can use it for his own personal benefit. He can turn the stones into bread, or gold, or any thing else he may desire; the riches of the world are his. He can carry out the wish of his boyhood, the dream of his youth, and the desire of his young manhood. He can startle his countrymen by stupendous miracles. He can pose as a conqueror. He can fill the *rôle* of king and ruler of the world; the power is his, and the prophecies apparently demand it. How shall he use this power?

Gradually, as light is given him, the real nature of the rule or kingdom of God dawns upon his mind. It is a kingdom not of this earth, but a spiritual kingdom. It is a new life, a new being, and the revealing of this new life, the requirements of this new being. How should he proclaim it? How would it be received? Would his countrymen be ready to give up the long-expected rule of their nation? would they abandon their desire for revenge, and renounce their dream of the glorious reign of Christ over the whole earth? How hard indeed was it to look these matters in the face, — to see the right course, and then pursue it!

Crushing all his own glowing hopes and aspirations, his dreams of glory, pomp, and power, and at the same time seeing the aversion, the disappointment, the disgust, with which his claim of being the Messiah would be received, unless accompanied with the evidences of earthly power and glory, he resolves upon his course of action. As the subject enlarges, and he sees clearer the course of events, he realizes his situation. A loving and compassionate spirit, yearning for love and companionship, he sees in himself a lonely and desolate man, despised, taunted, and rejected with scorn and anger by his own townsmen; without a place to lay his head, weary and heart-sick; his claim of being the Christ, although supported by miracles, rejected by the nation at large. He sees himself reviled by the learned men and the priests, to whom he had been taught to look up; the subject of scorn and contumely; even while using his power of miracle to relieve suffering, this very power credited to Satan, and he himself declared to be in collusion with evil spirits; followed by a few ignorant but loving men, who, while they attach themselves to him as his friends and disciples, still have a confused idea that he will soon proclaim himself as king and commence his reign; he sees himself in his great day of trial deserted even by his disciples, and left alone to meet a violent, painful, and disgraceful death, surrounded by scoffers, with the enemies of his nation taunting him and glorying in his sufferings.

Such are the scenes that reveal themselves to his awakened perceptions. Must he choose this way? Is there no other way? Must he not only give up his dreams of earthly splendor as the ruler of the world? but must he also take this path of humiliation, suffering, and disgraceful and violent death?

Can we wonder at the time taken, — the days and nights of prayer and conflict before the warfare ceased, and the decision was made? Was ever any man tempted like unto this man?

The long agony is over. The struggle between the desires, inclinations, hopes, and wishes of Jesus of Nazareth, the Son of man, born and educated to rule the world as an earthly king and conqueror, and the duties and responsibilities of Jesus the Christ, the anointed Son of God, has ceased; he has decided, and taken his stand. "Thou shalt worship the Lord thy God, and him only shalt thou serve," is his final answer to all these temptations. Jesus the Christ has conquered, and thereby has become the well-beloved Son of the most high God.

Jesus the Christ appears, clothed with more than mortal power, yet meek and lowly in spirit. He has deliberately made his choice, has turned his back on every thing connected with the earthly rule of his nation, and uses his power (which, if he had chosen earthly rule and sway, would have been shown in miracles like unto those of Moses and Joshua) to relieve suffering and distress. He goes about healing the sick and afflicted, and at the same time proclaims the coming of the kingdom of heaven, which, he teaches, is the rule of God in the heart, the love of God and man. We see him worn with toil, heart-sick at the evil around him, and the spiritual blindness of those with whom he comes in contact; we see him tried, and, though his judge acknowledges his innocence, we see him consigned to an ignominious and disgraceful death. We see also his resurrection, and his final departure from earth to heaven.

Jesus of Nazareth, in the struggle in the wilderness, realized what was required of him: that all this preparation of two thousand years had been for a purpose, and that purpose was to give unto man the evangel of God; that, through this evangel, man should obtain a knowledge of the Deity, and of his being and requirements, of eternal life, and the means by which it might be obtained.

Jesus was a man, a free agent. Like you or me, he had to make a decision. Good and evil were before him. Which should he choose?

The one way led to riches, honor, and worldly greatness. By the use of the miraculous power placed unreservedly in his hands, he could bring all nations to his feet, and become, what his imagination had sometimes pictured, the monarch of the world. He could give his friends untold riches, and make them great and prosperous. In so doing, he would fulfil the expectatious of his countrymen, and place the Hebrew nation on a pinacle of greatness, according with the apparent and generally believed prophecies respecting the Messiah.

The other way required the giving-up of all his long-cherished hopes and expectations, his desire for the happiness of his nation and the gratification of their wishes. It led to a life of self-denial, of self-abnegation, of sorrow, of ignominy; to a struggle against not only his own desires, but also against the hopes and expectations, the fierce wishes, of his nation, and even of those whom he should select as his friends and companions. It led to the utterance of doctrines which would be rejected by his nation, and misunderstood by his friends; and to a repulsive, painful, and ignominious death by the hands of the public executioner, deserted by his friends, and derided by his enemies.

Look on the two pictures, and say what temptation was ever like that which assailed this man during the forty days of his trial in the wilderness.

As we have never been tried like this man, and have never overcome like him, we can with all humility approach the Deity in his name, and as his disciples, endeavoring to follow his example, honoring him as the means whereby the evangel of God was again given to man through his teaching and suffering.

. . . .

We have reverently traced the footsteps of the Deity in his "plan of salvation," in his endeavor to save man from longer spiritual ignorance, and bring him again to himself. We have seen him as a household god select a member of the Semitic race, separate him from his kindred, gain his faith and trust and that of his immediate descendants, and cause them to settle in Egypt, there keeping them a separate people until they had increased to millions. Then, as Jehovah, we have seen him, by the exercise of his power, bring them out of bondage, and form them into a nation who of their own free will choose him as their national god.

We have seen the gradual advance of that nation in religious knowledge; and, in punishment of their many revolts against their god, have seen them carried captive into many lands. We have seen them advanced to offices of trust and honor in the great centres of civilization, and have seen the knowledge of Jehovah carried by them into every land.

All these were various steps necessary to prepare the world to receive a greater, fuller, more spiritual religion than any then known.

When, in the fulness of time, the world was ready to again receive the evangel formerly delivered to the Aryas, the messenger of the Deity for whose advent all this preparation had been made appeared.

In the New Testament, or New Contract, we can find this (to the world) new revelation, in all essential respects the first revelation repeated.

IV.

THE CLAIM OF JESUS OF NAZARETH TO BE THE CHRIST.

IN our first volume we have shown that God moves in the affairs of men; that the Aryas, the most highly organized race created by God, enclosed for thousands of years in the Garden of Eden, free from interruption from other races, there taught of God, and brought to a higher spiritual position than any other race has yet obtained, — that this race, when brought into temptation by commerce with other nations, by riches, and by almost universal rule, gradually fell from their high estate, neglected the task imposed upon them by the Deity, became sensuous and vile, and as a nation were swept by God from the face of the earth, but as a race were preserved by long-previous migrations.

In this volume we have traced the progress of the Deity in isolating the Israelites, and from them forming a nation through whose glory and shame, through whose successes and adversities, through miracles and prophecy, and through whose religious faithfulness in the end, a knowledge of God as Jehovah was spread abroad, and their belief in and expectation of a Messiah was made known throughout the civilized world. We have in the New Testament a record of the appearance, life, teachings, death, and resurrection of Jesus of Nazareth, who claimed to be the Christ, and for the truth of his claim referred to the prophecies, to the testimony of his parents, of God, of John the Baptist, and of his miracles.

Inasmuch as the Christ has been robbed of his distinction as the great exemplar and pattern for humanity, dethroned from the position of the greatest, the most virtuous man that ever existed, and deprived of his temptations, that greatest test of character, by theologians who have transformed him into a god, and thus taken from him his preeminence as the perfect man; and as others, misled by German criticism and free thought, deny the existence of the Christ, and claim that Jesus of Nazareth usurped a title which did not belong to him, and thereafter lived a life of deceit and fraud, — we propose to bring forward in the following pages the principal proofs on the points above referred to, and also to examine the teachings of this Christ, to see in what manner they differ (if at all) from those of the first revelation.

In making this examination, we must bear in mind the difference in the circumstances and surroundings of and in the race to whom these revelations were made. That the first revelation was given to a race slowly emerging from the animal nature, through social and intellectual knowledge, to the spiritual. That in their slow growth and isolated position, they had no knowledge of or belief in any other god to unlearn. That one only god was taught them. That having no outside influences to confuse them, every step in advance was assured and certain; and, as a result, we have the first and greatest revelation given to man.

The Christ came to a race naturally earthy, less spiritual; to a nation believing in many gods, but in his time loyal to their own national god. He came when certain beliefs and non-beliefs were prevalent and deeply seated, and not to be removed by the teachings of any individual, though he might have miraculous powers.

Under these circumstances the Christ was limited in his utterances with regard to the fatherhood of God, the sonship of man, the being of Satan, the existence of hell, the fate of the unenlightened, and on many other points. As in God's dealings with Abraham, and with Moses and the Israelites, he met them on the plane of *their* beliefs; so now the Christ met the Jews on the plain of *their* beliefs, and used them in enforcing and illustrating his own teachings.

MESSIANIC PROPHECIES.

The Jews, at the time of the appearance of Jesus of Nazareth as the Christ, were expecting the coming of a Messiah. This expectation was based upon prophecies recorded in the Hebrew scriptures, some of which are as follows:—

Abraham received this promise:—

"And in thy seed shall all the nations of the earth be blessed." (Gen. xxii. 18.)

Moses, in his last address to the Hebrews, says,—

"The Lord thy God will raise up unto thee a prophet from the midst of thee, of thy brethren, like unto me." (Deut. xviii. 15.)

Isaiah prophesies, "And in that day there shall be a root of Jesse, which shall stand for an ensign of the people; to it shall the Gentiles seek: and his rest shall be glorious." (Isa. xi. 10.)

Jeremiah, years afterwards, records the following: "Behold, the days come, saith the Lord, that I will raise unto David a righteous branch, and a king shall reign and prosper, and shall execute judgment and justice in the earth." (Jer. xxiii. 5.)

The Jews believed the time of the coming of the Christ was indicated in the prophecy of Daniel : —

"Know therefore and understand, that from the going forth of the commandment to restore and to build Jerusalem unto the Messiah the Prince shall be seven weeks, and threescore and two weeks." (Dan. ix. 25.)

These they understood to be weeks of years, each week indicating seven years. Seven weeks and sixty-two weeks are sixty-nine, and seven times sixty-nine are four hundred and eighty-three years.

The "going forth of the commandment" or order to rebuild *Jerusalem*, was given by Artaxerxes first in the twentieth year of his reign, or 445 B.C.; and Nehemiah was sent to carry out the order of the king. Eleven years previously this same king had sent Ezra to rebuild the *Temple* at Jerusalem.

The prophecy of Daniel says that the Messiah shall appear in four hundred and eighty-three years from the date of the order given by Artaxerxes to rebuild Jerusalem, which would make the year A.D. 38 the time for the anointing of, or for the appearance of, the Christ. Luke, the only one who speaks of the age of Jesus when he was anointed by the Holy Spirit, says, "And the Holy Ghost descended in a bodily shape like a dove upon him, and a voice came from heaven which said, Thou art my beloved Son, in thee I am well pleased. And Jesus himself began to be about thirty years of age." As there is an uncertainty with regard to A.D.,[1] as also the statement of age is "about," we may consider that the prophecy of Daniel was fulfilled to the letter, not at the *birth* of Jesus of Nazareth, but at his anointing; it was *that* which made him the Christ. The title of "Christ" did not belong to him until he was selected, appointed, commissioned, anointed, by the Holy Spirit.

The place of the birth of the Christ is also indicated: —

"But thou, Bethlehem Ephratah, though thou be little among the thousands of Judah, yet out of thee shall he come forth unto me that is to be ruler in Israel." (Mic. v. 2.)

The character and mission of the Christ are described as follows: —

"The Spirit of the Lord shall rest upon him, the spirit of wisdom and understanding, the spirit of counsel and might, the spirit of knowledge and of the fear of the Lord; and shall make him of

---

[1] Professor J. H. Allen of Harvard University, in his Hebrew Men and Times, places the enrolment for taxation, which was the cause for Joseph and Mary's journey to Bethlehem, as occurring in A.D. 7. This would coincide with the anointing of Jesus and his appearance as the Christ when he was thirty-one years old.

quick understanding in the fear of the Lord: and he shall not judge after the sight of his eyes, neither reprove after the hearing of his ears; but with righteousness shall he judge the poor, and reprove with equity for the meek of the earth: and he shall smite the earth with the rod of his mouth, and with the breath of his lips shall he slay the wicked; and righteousness shall be the girdle of his loins, and faithfulness the girdle of his reins." (Isa. xi. 2–5.)

Jesus, as the Christ, quotes and applies to himself the following: —

"The Spirit of the Lord God is upon me, because the Lord hath anointed me to preach good tidings unto the meek; he hath sent me to bind up the broken-hearted, to proclaim liberty to the captives, and the opening of the prison to them that are bound; to proclaim the acceptable year of the Lord." (Isa. lxi. 1, 2.)

It was also prophesied of the Christ, that he should perform miracles.

"Then the eyes of the blind shall be opened, and the ears of the deaf shall be unstopped; then shall the lame man leap as a hart, and the tongue of the dumb sing." (Isa. xxxv. 5, 6.)

There are also prophecies of a different character, to which, with the knowledge we have of the mission of the Christ, we give a meaning differing from the Jewish ideas and belief: —

"Of the increase of his government and peace there shall be no end, upon the throne of David and upon his kingdom, to order it, and to establish it with judgment and with justice from henceforth even forever. The zeal of the Lord of hosts will perform this." (Isa. ix. 7.)

"They shall serve the Lord their God, and David their king, whom I will raise up unto them." (Jer. xxx. 9.)

"And I the Lord will be their God, and my servant David a prince among them; I the Lord have spoken it." (Ezek. xxxiv. 24.)

"And David my servant shall be king over them, and they all shall have one shepherd: they shall also walk in my judgments, and observe my statutes, and do them: and they shall dwell in the land that I have given unto Jacob my servant, wherein your fathers have dwelt; and they shall dwell therein, even they, and their children, and their children's children forever: and my servant David shall be their prince forever." (Ezek. xxxvii. 24, 25.)

"I saw in the night visions, and, behold, one like the Son of man came with the clouds of heaven, and came to the Ancient of days, and they brought him near before him; and there was given him dominion, and glory, and a kingdom, that all people, nations, and languages should serve him: his dominion is an everlasting dominion, which shall not pass away, and his kingdom that which shall not be destroyed." (Dan. vii. 13, 14.)

The prophecies teem with visions of the glory, majesty, pomp, power, and universal and eternal rule of the expected Messiah. When we consider the general ignorance of the Jews of any spiritual requirements, their low conception of God, their belief in earthly rewards and punishments, and their expectation that because of their careful and punctilious performance of the requirements of the law of Moses since their deliverance from Babylonian bondage they would be rewarded by worldly success, — we can easily see that these glorious prophecies would be received and believed by them in their letter, and not in their spirit. The kingdom was to be an earthly kingdom; the ruler was to be another David, who was to inaugurate a new government, much more glorious than the original. To him all the nations of the earth should pay homage, and to his kingdom there should be no end.

We have seen the prophecies of the Messiah. Were they fulfilled in Jesus of Nazareth?

The Christ was to be of the seed of Abraham. That is not disputed.

He was to be a man "from the midst of you, like unto me," says Moses.

In support of this we have the records of his birth and of his youth, testified to by unimpeachable witnesses.

He was to be of the root of Jesse and of the line of David. This is testified to in both genealogies, — the one in Matthew reckoning down from Abraham, and the one in Luke reckoning up to Adam.

The prophecy of Daniel required the appearance of Messiah the Prince, four hundred and eighty-three years from the time the order to build Jerusalem was given to Nehemiah. We know the Jews, at the time of Christ, were impatiently awaiting his coming; and the time of his appearance was very near, if not at the exact date, of the prophecy. Jesus was about thirty years of age when he proclaimed himself to be the Messiah, apparently one year before the completion of the prophetic time.

The Christ was to be born in Bethlehem. We give herewith the testimony upon that point recorded by Matthew and Luke, of the birth of Jesus, with the accompanying incidents.

JESUS OF NAZARETH.

Mary, the mother of Jesus, testified, as recorded by Luke, that she was a "virgin espoused to a man whose name was Joseph, of the house of

David; and the angel came in unto her, and said, Hail, thou that art highly favored, the Lord is with thee; blessed art thou among women. And when she saw him she was troubled at his saying, and cast in her mind what manner of salutation this should be. And the angel said unto her, Fear not, Mary; for thou hast found favor with God; and behold, thou shalt conceive in thy womb, and bring forth a son, and shalt call his name Jesus. He shall be great, and shall be called the son of the Highest; and the Lord God shall give unto him the throne of his father David, and he shall reign over the house of Israel forever, and of his kingdom there shall be no end. Then Mary said unto the angel, How shall this thing be, seeing I know not a man? and the angel answered unto her, The Holy Ghost shall come upon thee, and the power of the Highest shall overshadow thee; therefore also that holy thing which shall be born of thee shall be called the Son of God. . . . And Mary said, Behold the handmaid of the Lord; be it unto me according to thy word. And the angel departed from her."

The testimony of Joseph, as recorded by Matthew: —

"When Mary was espoused to Joseph, before they had come together, she was found with child of the Holy Ghost. Then Joseph her husband, being a just man, and not willing to make her a public example, was minded to put her away privily. But while he thought on these things, behold, the angel of the Lord appeared unto him in a dream, saying, Joseph, thou son of David, fear not to take unto thee Mary thy wife: for that which is conceived in her is of the Holy Ghost. And she shall bring forth a son; and thou shalt call his name Jesus; for he shall save his people from their sins. . . . Then Joseph being raised from sleep, did as the angel of the Lord had bidden him, and took unto him his wife: and knew her not till she had brought forth her firstborn son: and he called his name Jesus."

The testimony of Joseph (additional) as reported by Luke:—

"And Joseph went up from Galilee, out of the city of Nazareth, to Judæa, unto the city of David, which is called Bethlehem; to be taxed, with Mary his espoused wife, being great with child. And while they were there, the days were accomplished that she should be delivered. And she brought forth her firstborn son, and wrapped him in swaddling clothes, and laid him in a manger, because there was no room for them in the inn."

The testimony of the shepherds as recorded by Luke:—

"And there were in the same country shepherds abiding in the field, keeping watch over their flocks by night. And lo, the angel of the Lord came upon them, and the glory of the Lord shone round about them: and they were sore afraid. And the angel said unto them, Fear not, for behold, I bring you good tidings of great joy, which shall be to all people: for unto you is born this day in the city of David, a Saviour, which is Christ the Lord. And this shall be a sign unto you: ye shall find the babe wrapped in swaddling clothes, and lying in a manger. And suddenly there was with the angel a multitude of the heavenly host, praising God, and saying, Glory to God in the highest, and on earth peace, good-will toward men. And it came to pass, as the angels were gone away from them into heaven, the shepherds said one to another, Let us now go even unto Bethlehem, and see this thing which is come to pass, which the Lord hath made known to us. And they came with haste, and found Mary and Joseph, and the babe lying in a manger. And when they had seen it, they made known abroad the saying which was told them concerning this child. And all they that heard it wondered at those things which were told them by the shepherds. But Mary kept all these things, and pondered them in her heart. And the shepherds returned, glorifying and praising God for all the things that they had heard and seen, as it was told unto them."

Testimony of Luke: —

"And when eight days were accomplished for the circumcising of the child, his name was called Jesus, which was so named of the angel before he was conceived in the womb. And when the days of the purification according to the law of Moses were accomplished, they brought him to Jerusalem to present him to the Lord, and to offer a sacrifice according to that which is said in the law of the Lord, A pair of turtle-doves or two young pigeons."

Testimony of Simeon, as recorded by Luke: —

"There was a man in Jerusalem whose name was Simeon: and the same man was just and devout, waiting for the consolation of Israel: and the Holy Ghost was upon him. And it was revealed to him by the Holy Ghost, that he should not see death before he had seen the Lord's Christ. And he came by the Spirit into the temple: and when the parents brought in the child Jesus, to do for him after the custom of the law, then took he him up in his arms, and blessed God, and said, Lord, now lettest thou thy servant depart in peace, according to thy word: for mine eyes have seen thy salvation, which thou hast prepared before the face of all people, a light to lighten the Gentiles, and the glory of thy people Israel."

The incidental testimony of the wise men, as recorded by Matthew : —

"Now when Jesus was born in Bethlehem of Judæa in the days of Herod the king, behold, there came wise men from the east to Jerusalem, saying, Where is he that is born King of the Jews? for we have seen his star in the east, and have come to worship him.

"When Herod the king had heard these things, he was troubled, and all Jerusalem with him; and when he had gathered all the chief priests and scribes of the people together, he demanded of them where Christ should be born. And they said unto him, In Bethlehem of Judæa: for thus it is written by the prophet: And thou Bethlehem, in the land of Juda, art not least among the princes of Juda; for out of thee shall come a Governor, that shall rule my people Israel. Then Herod, when he had privily called the wise men, inquired of them diligently what time the star appeared. And he sent them to Bethlehem, and said, Go and search diligently for the young child; and when ye have found him, bring me word again, that I may come and worship him also.

"When they had heard the king, they departed; and, lo, the star, which they saw in the east, went before them, till it came and stood over where the young child was. When they saw the star, they rejoiced with exceeding great joy. And when they were come into the house, they saw the young child with Mary his mother, and fell down, and worshipped him: and when they had opened their treasures, they presented unto him gifts; gold, frankincense, and myrrh. And being warned of God in a dream that they should not return to Herod, they departed into their own country another way."

THE CHRIST.

"The Spirit of the Lord" was to rest upon him. He himself claims that "The Spirit of the Lord God is upon me, because the Lord hath anointed me." This claim is supported by the testimony of the voice from heaven, as given by Matthew, Mark, and Luke:—

"And Jesus, when he was baptized, went up straightway out of the water: and, lo, the heavens were opened unto him, and he saw the Spirit of God descending like a dove, and lighting upon him: and lo a voice from heaven saying, This is my beloved Son, in whom I am well pleased."

The testimony of John the Baptist, to the same event, as recorded by the Apostle John:—

"And this is the record of John, when the Jews sent priests and Levites from Jerusalem to ask him, Who art thou? And he confessed, and denied not; but confessed, I am not the Christ." "The next day John seeth Jesus coming unto him, and saith, Behold the Lamb of God, which taketh away the sin of the world. This is he of whom I said, After me cometh a man which is preferred before me: for he was before me. And I knew him not: but that he should be made manifest to Israel, therefore am I come baptizing with water. And John bare record, saying, I saw the Spirit descending from heaven like a dove, and it abode upon him. And I knew him not; but he that sent me to baptize with water, the same said unto me, Upon whom thou shalt see the Spirit descending, and remaining on him, the same is he which baptizeth with the Holy Ghost. And I saw, and bare record that this is the Son of God.

"Again the next day after, John stood, and two of his disciples; and looking upon Jesus as he walked, he saith, Behold the Lamb of God!"

Testimony of the voice from heaven at a later period, as recorded by Matthew, Mark, and Luke: —

"And after six days Jesus taketh Peter, James, and John his brother, and bringeth them up into a high mountain apart, and was transfigured before them: and his face did shine as the sun, and his raiment was white as the light. And, behold, there appeared unto them Moses and Elias talking with him. Then answered Peter, and said unto Jesus, Lord, it is good for us to be here: if thou wilt, let us make here three tabernacles; one for thee, and one for Moses, and one for Elias. While he yet spake, behold, a bright cloud overshadowed them; and behold a voice out of the cloud, which said, This is my beloved Son, in whom I am well pleased; hear ye him."

We see that by the testimony of unimpeachable witnesses, the requirements in the prophecies of the Christ, regarding the place of his birth, were fulfilled in the birth and consecration of Jesus of Nazareth. And in addition we have the indorsement of the angels and shepherds, of Simeon and Anna, and of the wise men, as to his birth; of John the Baptist, and the voice from heaven, as to his consecration.

THE SON OF GOD.

Jesus of Nazareth, the Son of God, claimed to be the Christ, the *anointed* Son of Jehovah, the long-expected Messiah of the Jews. He said that God had selected and chosen him for a specific purpose, to do a specific work; that he acted wholly as his agent and representative; that what he said was spoken by his direction, and what he did was done by the power God had placed in his hands.

In the temptations in the wilderness, he showed that he was, and felt himself to be, a free agent, as he had always been; and free to act as he thought best, as are all the sons of God. He accepted the mission of his own free will, and his course of action was decided by himself. He claimed that his teachings fulfilled, or filled out and completed, the laws of Moses; that what he taught was by revelation from God; and on that ground he claimed from others faith in himself and belief in the truth and authority of the doctrines he enunciated.

For proof that he was the Son of God, the anointed, as expected by the Jews, he referred to the testimony of God, of John the Baptist, and especially to the miracles performed by him, as being of a nature carrying with them God's approval, as they could not be performed without his consent and aid. His knowledge of God, — of his being, relationship, and purposes, — he claimed to have received directly from God himself; and the power of miracle which he possessed and used, he constantly referred to God, that of himself he could do nothing.

Having by his miracles established the fact that he was a son of God endowed with extraordinary powers, thereby becoming, by way of distinction, *the* Son of God, he proceeded to reveal the Deity, not as the household or personal God of Abraham, Isaac, and Jacob; nor as Jehovah, the tutelary God of the Hebrew nation; but as our Father, the one and only God, Maker of the universe, and the Father of the whole human race, who he declared were brothers, sons of the one universal Father. He revealed the love of God for man, and promulgated the law of love to God and man as the fulfilling of the law. He also taught of the resurrection of the dead, and of a future life; and in his death, resurrection, and ascension, gave proof of the truth of his teaching.

Jesus took up the cry of John the Baptist, and proclaimed the kingdom of heaven to be at hand; that is, the laws, the rule, or government, of God were at hand, about to be proclaimed and taught. The kingdom of heaven is a government, and those who would obtain eternal life must vow allegiance to that government, and obey its laws. These laws of the kingdom, Jesus, as the Christ, revealed; and the apostles journeyed into all lands, proclaiming this kingdom, promulgating the fact of eternal life, and teaching men how to obtain it.

We will see what proof we have in the New Testament to support the claim that he was the Christ, the anointed Son of God, and that he was endowed with extraordinary power and knowledge by God, for the purposes of his mission. In so doing we will cite both the statements of Jesus himself, and collateral evidence.

"Jesus saith unto them, But whom say *ye* that I am? And Simon Peter answered and said, Thou art the Christ, the Son of the living God. And Jesus answered and said, Blessed art thou, Simon Bar-Jonah: for flesh and blood hath not revealed it unto thee, but my Father which is in heaven." (Mark viii. 29; and Luke ix. 20.)

"Jesus heard that they had cast him out; and when he had found him he said unto him, Dost thou believe on the Son of God? He answered and said, Who is he, Lord, that I may believe on him? And Jesus said unto him, Thou hast both seen him, and it is he that talketh with thee." (John ix. 37.)

"When Jesus heard that, he said, This sickness is not unto death, but for the glory of God, that the Son of God might be glorified thereby." (John xi. 4.)

"Jesus walked in the temple in Solomon's porch. Then came the Jews round about him, and said unto him, How long dost thou make us to doubt? If thou be the Christ, tell us plainly. Jesus answered them, I told you, and ye believed not: the works that I do in my Father's name, they bear witness of me." (John x. 23.)

"If I bear witness of myself, my witness is not true: there is another that beareth witness of me, and I know that the witness which he witnesseth of me is true. Ye sent unto John, and he bare witness unto the truth. . . . But I have greater witness than that of John: for the works which the Father hath given me to finish, the same works that I do, bear witness of me, that the Father hath sent me. And the Father himself, which hath sent me, hath borne witness of me." (John v. 31–33, 36, 37.)

"It is also written in your law, that the testimony of two men is true. I am one that bear witness of myself, and the Father that sent me beareth witness of me." (John viii. 17, 18.)

"And John calling unto him two of his disciples sent them to Jesus, saying, Art thou he that should come? or look we for another? . . . Then Jesus answering said unto them, Go your way, and tell John what things ye have seen and heard; how that the blind see, the lame walk, the lepers are cleansed, the deaf hear, the dead are raised, to the poor the gospel is preached." (Luke vii. 19, 22.)

"Say ye of him whom the Father hath sanctified, and sent into the world, Thou blasphemest; because I said, I am the Son of God? If I do not the works of my Father, believe me not. But if I do, though ye believe not me, believe the works." (John x. 36-38.)

"Then said they all, Art thou the Son of God? And he said unto them, Ye say that I am." (Luke xxii. 70.)

"And the high priest said unto him, I adjure thee by the living God, that thou tell us whether thou be the Christ, the Son of God. Jesus saith unto him, Thou hast said." (Matt. xxvi. 64.)

"As the Father gave me commandment, even so I do." (John xiv. 28.)

"I have kept my Father's commandments, and abide in his love." (John xv. 10.)

"I go unto the Father, for my Father is greater than I." (John xiv. 28.)

"Therefore doth my Father love me, because I lay down my life, that I might take it again. No man taketh it from me, but I lay it down of myself: I have power to lay it down, and I have power to take it again. This commandment [or this power] have I received of my Father." (John x. 17.)

"I came forth from the Father, and am come into the world: again, I leave the world, and go to the Father." (John xvi. 28.)

"Then said Jesus unto them, When ye have lifted up the Son of man, then shall ye know that

I am he, and that I do nothing of myself; but as my Father hath taught me, I speak these things." (John viii. 28.)

"Verily I say unto you, Whatsoever ye shall ask the Father in my name, he will give it you." (John xvi. 23.)

"I came forth from the Father, and am come into the world." (John xvi. 28.)

"All things are delivered unto me of my Father; and no man knoweth the Son but the Father; and neither knoweth any man the Father, save the Son, and he to whomsoever the Son will reveal him." (Luke x. 22.)

"The words I speak unto you, I speak not of myself; but the Father that dwelleth in me, he doeth the works." (John xiv. 16.)

"For I have not spoken of myself; but the Father which sent me, he gave me a commandment, what I should say, and what I should speak." (John xii. 49.)

"The word which ye hear is not mine, but the Father's which sent me." (John xiv. 24.)

"For as the Father hath life in himself, so hath he given to the Son to have life in himself; and hath given him authority to execute judgment also, because he is the Son of man." (John v. 26, 27.)

"The Son can do nothing of himself, but what

he seeth the Father do; for what things soever he doeth, these also doeth the Son likewise." (John v. 19.)

"For as the Father raiseth up the dead, and quickeneth them, even so the Son quickeneth whom he will: for the Father judgeth no man, but hath committed all judgment unto the Son; that all men should honor the Son, even as they honor the Father. He that honoreth not the Son honoreth not the Father which hath sent him." (John v. 21–23.)

"The Father is in me, and I in him." (John x. 38.)

"My Father is greater than I." (John xiv. 28.)

"All things that I have heard of my Father, I have made known unto you." (John xv. 15.)

"I speak that which I have seen with my Father." (John viii. 38.)

"If I do not the works of my Father, believe me not." (John x. 37.)

"All things that the Father hath are mine." (John xvi. 15.)

"Again I say unto you, That if two of you shall agree on earth as touching any thing that they shall ask, it shall be done for them of my Father which is in heaven." (Matt. xviii. 19.)

"And whatsoever ye shall ask in my name, that will I do; that the Father may be glorified in the Son." (John xiv. 13.)

"Jesus saith unto him, I am the way, the truth, and the life: no man cometh unto the Father, but by me." (John xiv. 6.)

"I give unto them eternal life; and they shall never perish, neither shall any man pluck them out of my hand. My Father which gave them me, is greater than all; and no man is able to pluck them out of my Father's hand. I and my Father are one." (John x. 28–30.)

"Not every one that saith unto me, Lord, Lord, shall enter into the kingdom of heaven; but he that doeth the will of my Father which is in heaven." (Matt. vii. 21.)

"Whosoever therefore shall confess me before men, him will I confess also before my Father which is in heaven; but whosoever shall deny me before men, him will I also deny before my Father which is in heaven." (Matt. x. 32, 33.)

"At that time Jesus answered and said, I thank thee, O Father, Lord of heaven and earth, because thou hast hid these things from the wise and prudent, and hast revealed them unto babes. Even so, Father; for so it seemed good in thy sight." (Matt. xi. 25.)

"I judge no man; and yet if I judge, my judgment is true; for I am not alone, but I and the Father that sent me." (John viii. 15.)

"For the Father judgeth no man, but hath committed all judgment unto the Son." (John v. 22.)

"Verily, verily, I say unto you, He that heareth my word, and believeth on him that sent me, hath everlasting life, and shall not come into condemnation, but is passed from death to life. . . . The hour is coming, and now is, when the dead shall hear the voice of the Son of God, and they that hear shall live. For as the Father hath life in himself, so hath he given to the Son to have life in himself, and hath given him authority to execute judgment also; because he is the Son of man." (John v. 24–27.)

CORROBORATIVE TESTIMONY.

The testimony of the Jews as recorded by John:—

"The Jews answered and said, We have a law, and by our law he ought to die, because he made himself the Son of God." (John xix. 7.)

Nathaniel's belief, as recorded by John:—

"Nathaniel answered and said unto him, Rabbi, thou art the Son of God." (John i. 49.)

Simon Peter says in the name of the twelve disciples, "We believe and are sure that thou art that Christ, the Son of the living God." (John vi. 69.)

Simon Peter's belief, as recorded by Matthew and John:—

"Simon Peter answered and said, Thou art the Christ, the Son of the living God."

The belief of the disciples, as recorded by John:—

"We believe that thou camest forth from God." (John xvi. 30.)

The belief of the people, as recorded by Matthew:—

"Then they that were in the ship came and worshipped him, saying, Of a truth thou art the Son of God." (Matt. xix. 13.)

Testimony of the chief priests, as recorded by Matthew:—

"The chief priests, mocking him, said, He trusted in God. Let him deliver him now, if he will have him; for he said, I am the Son of God." Matt. xxvii. 43.)

Belief of the centurion, as recorded by Matthew, Mark, and Luke:—

"And when the centurion, which stood over against him, saw that he so cried out, and gave up the ghost, he said, Truly this man was the Son of God." (Mark xv. 39.)

The belief of Mark, as recorded by himself:—

"The beginning of the gospel of Jesus Christ, the Son of God." (Mark i. 1.)

The belief of Peter, in the record of his words in Acts:—

"The God of our fathers hath glorified his Son Jesus." (Acts iii. 13.)

"Unto you first, God having raised up his Son Jesus, sent him to bless you." (Acts iii. 26.)

"Therefore let all the house of Israel know assuredly, that God hath made that same Jesus, whom ye have crucified, both Lord and Christ." (Acts ii. 36.)

Belief of John, as recorded in his writings:—

"And we have seen, and do testify, that the Father sent the Son to be the Saviour of the world." (John iv. 14.)

"And this is his commandment, That we should believe on the name of his Son Jesus Christ." (John iii. 23.)

"In this was manifested the love of God towards us, because that God sent his only begotten Son into the world, that we might live through him." (1 John iv. 9.)

"Whoever shall confess that Jesus is the Son of God, God dwelleth in him, and he in God." (1 John iv. 15.)

"For God so loved the world, that he gave his only begotten Son, that whosoever believeth in him should not perish, but have everlasting life." (John iii. 16.)

"But these are written that ye might believe that Jesus is the Christ, the Son of God." (John xx. 31.)

"Who is he that overcometh the world, but he that believeth that Jesus is the Son of God?" (1 John v. 5.)

"Our fellowship is with the Father, and with his Son Jesus Christ." (1 John i. 3.)

"Grace be with you, mercy and peace from God the Father, and from the Lord Jesus Christ, the Son of the Father in truth and love." (2 John i. 3.)

Belief of Paul, as recorded in his writings: —

"Paul, a servant of Jesus Christ, called to be an apostle, separated unto the gospel of God, concerning Jesus Christ our Lord, which was made of the seed of David according to the flesh, and declared to be the Son of God with power." (Rom. i. 1–4.)

"God, who at sundry times and in divers manners spake in times past unto the fathers by the prophets, hath in these last days spoken unto us by his Son." (Heb. i. 1, 2.)

"For the Son of God, Jesus Christ, who was preached among you by us." (2 Cor. i. 19.)

"God sending his own Son in the likeness of sinful flesh." (Rom. viii. 3.)

"I live by the faith of the Son of God, who loved me, and gave himself for me." (Gal. ii. 20.)

"He that spared not his own Son, but delivered him up for us all." (Rom. viii. 32.)

"We give thanks to God and the Father of our Lord Jesus Christ." (Col. i. 3.)

"But when the fulness of the time came, God sent forth his Son, born of a woman, born under the law, that he might redeem them which were under the law, that we might receive the adoption of sons; and because we are sons, God sent forth the Spirit of his Son into our hearts, crying, Abba, Father; so that thou art no longer a bondservant, but a son, and if a son, then an heir through God." (Gal. iv. 4–7.)

SON OF MAN.

Jesus, prevented by the belief of the Jews from proclaiming that all mankind were children of God, endeavored to familiarize the thought by indiscriminately describing himself as Son of God and son of man. We find that in both positions he claims the same power, and declares that his power is by the gift of God.

We have shown that Jesus of Nazareth was born at Bethlehem; that he was a babe born of a woman like all other human beings, that as a child he was like other children, as a boy he was like other boys; and that when he came to John to be baptized, he was a man like other men.

John the Baptist did not know Jesus as the Messiah, until he was revealed to him by the descent of the Holy Spirit. He was a relative; and from the intimacy of the mothers John had undoubtedly a personal acquaintance with him sufficient to give him a knowledge of the character of Jesus; and this is shown in his reluctance to baptize a man with the baptism of repentance, whose character he knew to be blameless. "He would have hindered him;" and he expresses this feeling, saying, "I have need to be baptized of thee, and comest thou to me?" And it is only at the earnest persuasion of Jesus, that he does baptize him.

We have no record showing that Jesus was different from other men in any way, until after his baptism; and after that event he still claims the position of a son of man, and speaks of himself as follows: —

"Who do men say that I the Son of man am?" (Matt. xvi. 13.)

"The Son of man hath not where to lay his head." (Matt. viii. 20.)

"The Son of man hath power to forgive sin." (Matt. ix. 6.)

"The Son of man came eating and drinking." (Matt. xi. 19.)

"The Son of man is lord of the sabbath." (Matt. xii. 8.)

"The Son of man must suffer many things." (Luke ix. 22.)

"Every one who shall confess me before men, him shall the Son of man confess before the angels of God." (Luke xii. 8.)

"Ye shall desire to see one of the days of the Son of man." (Luke xvii. 22.)

"For the Son of man came to seek and to save that which was lost." (Luke xix. 10.)

"It is written of the Son of man that he should suffer many things." (Mark ix. 12.)

"The Son of man is delivered up into the hands of men." (Mark ix. 31.)

"Judas, betrayest thou the Son of man with a kiss?" (Luke xxvii. 48.)

"Even the Son of man which is in heaven." (John iii. 13.)

"So must the Son of man be lifted up." (John iii. 14.)

"Because he is the Son of man." (John v. 27.)

"Jesus therefore said, When ye have lifted up the Son of man, then shall ye know that I am he." (John viii. 28.)

"And Jesus answered them, saying, The hour

is come that the Son of man should be glorified." (John xii. 23.)

"Jesus saith, Now is the Son of man glorified." (John xiii. 31.)

"When the Son of man should have arisen again from the dead." (Mark ix. 9.)

"What then, if ye should behold the Son of man ascending where he was before." (John vi. 62.)

"The meat which abideth unto eternal life, which the Son of man shall give unto you." (John vi. 27.)

"But when the Son of man shall come in his glory." (Matt. xxv. 31.)

"Whosoever therefore shall be ashamed of me and my words in this adulterous and sinful generation, of him also shall the Son of man be ashamed when he cometh in the glory of his Father with the holy angels." (Mark viii. 38.)

"Tell the vision to no man, until the Son of man be risen again from the dead." (Matthew, Mark.)

"For the Son of man shall come in the glory of his Father, with his angels." (Matt. xvi. 27.)

"Hereafter shall ye see the Son of man sitting on the right hand of power, and coming in the clouds of heaven." (Mark xiv. 62.)

"In such an hour as ye think not, the Son of man cometh." (Matt. xxiv. 44.)

"Watch therefore; for ye know neither the day nor the hour wherein the Son of man cometh." (Matt. xxv. 13.)

"But as the days of Noe, so shall also the coming of the Son of man be." (Matt. xxiv. 37.)

"For as the lightning cometh out of the east, and shineth even unto the west, so shall also the coming of the Son of man be." (Matt. xxiv. 27.)

"The Son of man shall send forth his angels." (Matt. xiii. 41.)

"When the Son of man shall come in his glory, and all the holy angels with him, then shall he sit upon the throne of his glory." (Matt. xxv. 31.)

"Then shall appear the sign of the Son of man in heaven; and then shall all the tribes of the earth mourn; and they shall see the Son of man coming in the clouds of heaven, with power and great glory; and he shall send his angels with a great sound of a trumpet, and they shall gather together his elect from the four winds, from one end of heaven to the other." (Mark, Luke.)

"Hereafter ye shall see heaven open, and the angels of God ascending and descending upon the Son of man." (John i. 51.)

Jesus, while claiming power beyond that of

man, still emphasizes the fact that he is a man, partaking of the nature of all men; that the extraordinary position given him by God does not alter the fact of his being a man, and tempted in all points as other men. His mother and brethren were known; his neighbors and townsmen say, " Whence hath this man this wisdom?" (Matt. xiii. 54.)

OTHER TESTIMONY.

His disciples, and the Jews generally, believe him to be a man.

" Howbeit we know this man, whence he is." (John vii. 27.)

"Never man spake like this man." (John vii. 46.)

" The man that is called Jesus made clay, and anointed my eyes." (John ix. 11.)

" The Jews cried out, If thou release this man." (John xix. 12.)

The apostles speak of Jesus as a man. Peter, in his first address on the Day of Pentecost, says, —

"Jesus of Nazareth, a man approved of God unto you by mighty works." (Acts ii. 22.)

" Be it known unto you therefore, brethren, that through this man is proclaimed unto you remission of sins." (Acts xiii. 38.)

" Stephen in his vision says, Behold, I see the

heavens opened, and the Son of man standing on the right hand of God." (Acts vii. 56.)

"It behooved him in all things to be made like unto his brethren; for in that he hath suffered, being tempted, he is able to succor them that are tempted." (Heb. ii. 18.)

"This man continueth ever." (Heb. vii. 24.)

Paul writes, "For there is one God, and one mediator between God and man, the man Christ Jesus." 1 Tim. ii. 5.)

Jesus of Nazareth, being a man like other men, was endowed with the Holy Spirit from God far beyond that of any other man previous or since, and became, by the act of God, his Anointed, his Messiah, his Christ. Moses, Joshua, Elijah, each had this power bestowed upon them. The prophets were enlightened as to future events; each received the Holy Spirit to a limited extent, sufficient for the position in which he was placed and the work he was called upon to do. Their power or enlightenment did not extend beyond the special object of their being; in all other respects they were men, showing the same individuality of character as other men.

The Holy Spirit was poured out upon Jesus without measure. In the great work he was called upon to perform, he was still a free agent: he could adopt any plan of operation he desired.

He has, in the slight glimpses he has given us of his temptations in the desert, shown some of the paths he might have taken; and in his life and death we see the path which he deliberately chose, and which he quietly and firmly trod to the end, ever pressing onward, seeing the end from the beginning, yet steadily pursuing the course he had at that time chosen. We can see the intensity of his feeling, when, tempted by Peter in the same way in which he had been tempted in the desert, he says to him, "Get thee behind me, Satan." This power to work his own will, he retained even unto the end; as shown by his remark in the garden of Gethsemane, "Thinkest thou that I cannot beseech my Father, and he shall even now send me more than twelve legions of angels?" So, too, he claims it to be of his own free will, that he goes to his death: "Therefore doth the Father love me, because I lay down my life that I may take it again. No one taketh it away from me, but I lay it down of myself. I have power to lay it down, and I have power to take it again." This power, he says, he received from the Father. Great as it was, it falls far short of the creative and energizing power of God, of his omniscience, omnipotence, and omnipresence, — powers claimed for the Christ by believers in him as God.

Jesus as a child, a youth, a young man, and a

man of mature years, had lived a life of peculiar and great temptation, as we have endeavored to show in the previous chapters of this work; and now as the Christ, the Messiah so long promised and desired, his temptations (providing he was a man, and not God, "for God cannot be tempted with evil") were still greater. To sustain him under these extraordinary temptations, he held frequent communion with God. As his earthly end approached, he was enlightened more and more as to the result of his work, strengthened by a knowledge of its final acknowledgment throughout the world, and by visions of his own position and power in the kingdom of heaven which he had established upon earth.

The attempts of evangelical Christians to deify Christ, have put him out of the plane of human existence. They have made him a God: and his human life, which was an example for man to follow, because he was a man, has been lost; and his teachings, which were so plain and simple that the most ignorant might understand, have been hidden, or so changed and obscured by this halo of deification as to take a symbolical form; and the great purposes of his life are lessened, and made of little value compared with the so-called work of redemption, which they declare was accomplished by the shedding of his blood as God upon the cross, — an act, which, if he was God, was a farce and a cheat, because God cannot put himself in the power of his creature man, and cannot die.

The simple death of a human being has been tortured into the sacrifice of God, and Christ the Son of man has been robbed of his birthright, and cheated out of the lessons of his life as an example for man; because, if he was God, he could not be tempted of evil, and could not therefore show unto man who is tempted the way to resist temptation, and overcome evil.

This deifying of Christ has been and is a great hinderance and stumbling-block to mankind. It has caused the manufacture by man of an elaborate scheme of salvation not found in the Christian Scriptures; it has caused the promulgation of creeds and doctrines entirely opposed to those of Christ, and has placed him on a pinnacle unapproachable by men, and made his life and example of no effect.

Christ's prayer in the garden of Gethsemane, "Father, if thou be willing, remove this cup from me; nevertheless not my will, but thine be done. . . . And being in agony, he prayed more earnestly: and his sweat was as it were great drops of blood falling down to the ground" (Luke xxii. 42–44), is the prayer, not of a God, but of a man, not fearful of death, but feeling strongly the ignominy, disgrace, and suffering connected therewith, desiring to be released from the ordeal, and praying to one who he knows has the power to remove the cup if he will. It is the agony of a man conscious of what he is about to undergo, and nervously shrinking from it, but who will, when the time comes, meet his fate calmly and with resignation.

"My God! My God! Why hast thou forsaken me?" is the cry of a man overcome by pain, for a moment losing his trust in God; the cry of one who would not use the power given him, to lessen his sufferings in the least, but leaving all in the hands of God.

"Father, into thy hands I commend my spirit," is the prayer of a loving, trusting human being, to his Father and his God; not the cry of one God to another, or of God to himself.

THE CHRIST'S MIRACLES.

Miracles exhibit a power beyond or overruling the laws of nature: they are exhibitions of the spiritual force, energy, or enlightening powers of God, which have been given to a limited extent by the Deity into the hands of man, that he may work out God's purposes.

We see this power used by Moses to free the

Israelites from bondage, and to keep control over the ignorant hordes of slaves set free; by Joshua, to conquer a country for the new nation; by occasional prophets, to keep alive the knowledge and worship of Jehovah. In all these cases, the power given was limited to the special purpose for which it was bestowed.

The Christ received this power without limit. "All power is given unto me in heaven and in earth," he says. That he could use it for his own personal benefit, or for that of his friends, is shown in the miracle at Cana in Galilee, and in his statement that if he wished he could have "twelve legions of angels" to protect or defend him. The immense power he used only to advance the purpose of his mission. He bestowed the power on his disciples; sending forth seventy at one time, who, on their return, testified to the efficacy of the power. The same power or influence was given to the apostles, including Barnabas and Paul.

As the Christ is our exemplar, the perfect man, whom we are to follow in all things, there is reason to believe that this supernatural power of the spirit, which was so freely given to him and his disciples, may be again given to man when he is ready to receive and use it in the spirit of the Christ.

The Jews believed that the Messiah would perform miracles; and Jesus frequently referred to his works, as evidence of the truth of his claim to be the Messiah.

The record of the Christ's miracles permeates the Gospels. Many of them have the testimony of two or more of the writers thereof, and they cannot be eliminated without destroying the whole work. The conversations and incidents connected with them are perfectly natural, and bear the impress of simplicity and truth.

Besides these records of specific miracles, we have the testimony of the apostles and others, showing the profusion of these acts, and that they were generally known and acknowledged by the Jews.

In answer to John the Baptist's inquiry sent through two of his disciples, "Art thou he that should come, or do we look for another?" Jesus answered and said unto them, "Go and show John again those things which ye do hear and see: the blind receive their sight, and the lame walk, the lepers are cleansed, and the deaf hear, the dead are raised up, and the poor have the gospel preached unto them." (Matt. xi. 4, 5.)

"But I have greater witness than that of John; for the works which the Father hath given me to finish, the same works that I do, bear witness of me, that the Father hath sent me." (John v. 36.)

"Jesus answered them, I told you, and ye believed not: the works that I do in my Father's name, they bear witness of me." (John x. 25.)

Jesus applies to himself the Messianic prophecy of Isaiah, "The Spirit of the Lord is upon me; because he hath anointed me to preach the gospel to the poor; he hath sent me to heal the brokenhearted, to preach deliverance to the captives, and recovering of sight to the blind, to set at liberty them that are bruised." (Luke iv. 18.)

The answer of Jesus to the centurion's request that he would heal his servant is, "I will come and heal him." (Matt. viii. 7.)

To the nobleman, who besought him to come down and heal his son, he says, "Go thy way: thy son liveth." (John iv. 50.)

Matthew testifies: —

"And great multitudes followed him, and he healed them all." (Matt. xii. 15.)

"John [the Baptist] heard in prison the works of Christ." (Matt. xi. 2.)

"And his fame went throughout all Syria: and they brought unto him all sick people that were taken with divers diseases and torments, and those which were possessed with devils, and those which were lunatic, and those that had the palsy; and he healed them." (Matt. iv. 24.)

"And Jesus went forth, and saw a great

multitude, and was moved with compassion toward them, and he healed their sick." (Matt. xiv. 14.)

"And great multitudes followed him, and he healed them all." (Matt. xii. 15.)

Luke testifies: —

"And it came to pass on a certain day, as he was teaching, that there were Pharisees and doctors of the law sitting by, which were come out of every town of Galilee, and Judæa, and Jerusalem; and the power of the Lord was present to heal them." (Luke v. 17.)

"And in the same hour he cured many of their infirmities and plagues, and of evil spirits: and unto many that were blind he gave sight." (Luke vii. 21.)

John testifies very fully: —

"Now when he [Jesus] was in Jerusalem, at the passover, in the feast day, many believed in his name, when they saw the miracles which he did." (John ii. 23.)

"And a great multitude followed him, because they saw his miracles which he did on them that were diseased." (John vi. 2.)

Nicodemus testifies, "Rabbi, we know that thou art a teacher come from God: for no man can do these miracles that thou doest, except God be with him." (John iii. 2.)

"Many of the people believed on him, and said, When Christ cometh, will he do more miracles than these which this man hath done?" (John vii. 31.)

"The Pharisees said, This man is not of God, because he keepeth not the sabbath day. Others said, How can a man that is a sinner do such miracles?" (John ix. 16.)

"Then gathered the chief priests and the Pharisees a council, and said, What do we? for this man doeth many miracles." (John xi. 47.)

Peter addresses the Jews as knowing of the miracles: he says, "Ye men of Israel, hear these words: Jesus of Nazareth, a man approved of God among you by miracles, wonders, and signs, which God did by him in the midst of you, as ye yourselves know." (Acts ii. 22.)

Paul, also, in his address to the Hebrews, says, "How shall we escape, if we neglect so great salvation? which at the first began to be spoken by the Lord, and was confirmed unto us by them that heard him; God also bearing them witness both with signs and wonders, and with diverse miracles." (Heb. ii. 34.)

Luke testifies of the Roman centurion who said, "I am not worthy that thou shouldest come under my roof; but speak the word only, and my servant shall be healed." (Matt. viii. 8; Luke vii. 10.)

John says of the nobleman whose son was sick at Capernaum, "Jesus saith unto him, Go thy way, thy son liveth. . . . So the father knew that it was the same hour in the which Jesus said unto him, Thy son liveth; and himself believed, and his whole house." (John iv. 53.)

PRE-EXISTENCE.

As we obtain larger and larger glimpses of creation, of the innumerable worlds existing, and of others in process of formation, and consider the smallness and insignificance of this earth as compared with other worlds of our own solar system, and that with countless other systems beyond, we feel that God has been working for millions upon millions of years, and that this earth is not the first, but among the latest, of his creations. We know that God does not work without an object, and we are certain that for these countless millions of ages before this earth was, the shining orbs above and around us have not been created without their use; and is it not probable that they are the abodes of intelligent beings, — beings who perhaps have been in existence for millions of years before this earth was created?

Of these things we know nothing, but our reason shows the probability of such a state of being. We know not but we may ourselves have lived in such a previous state of existence. The body shuts our sight to things past, and to things beyond. We may in some future state of existence be able to say with Christ, "I came from God; for neither have I come of myself, but he sent me."

We know nothing of any previous state of existence; neither did Christ, until enlightened by the Holy Spirit, even then not when he first received the blessing. If we can judge any thing by the records, he was gradually instructed, at first, with respect to his mission as the Messiah; his frequent communions with God not only strengthened him in the path he had chosen, but he was enlightened not only as to the position he would take as God's well-beloved Son in the kingdom of heaven, but, as we see, it also brought to him the knowledge of his pre-existence.

No one can tell when man, the spiritual being, enters and takes possession of the human body. Neither can we tell whence he comes, except from the one great source, God; whether this earth is his place of birth, or whether he has existed in other times and in other worlds. But as Christ existed before this world was, we may believe that some or all of us have had a pre-existence; but, pre-existent or not, we know that we are sons of God, even as Christ is Son of God, and that he is an example of what we may become.

Christ earnestly and repeatedly states that all his power is given unto him, that "The Son can do nothing of himself." "My teaching is not mine, but his that sent me." "He that sent me is true; and the things which I heard from him, these speak I unto you." How shall we reconcile these statements with other sayings, such as, "I and my Father are one;" "He that seeth me, seeth him that sent me;" "Believe me that I am in the Father, and the Father in me"?

The Christ claimed to be the sent of God, his anointed representative and agent.

The kingdoms and governments of this earth in times of exigency send ambassadors, called ministers plenipotentiary, to each other's courts, clothed with the power and authority of their governments. The United States, for instance, sends a minister plenipotentiary to the Court of St. James. He appears in Great Britain clothed in the power, the authority, the sovereignty, of the United States; he is the United States manifest in the flesh. As an official, his acts are the acts of the United States, his words are the words of the United States, his promises and threats are the promises and threats of the United States. He that hears him hears the United States, and he that sees him sees the United States.

In the same way the Christ was the ambassador,

the minister plenipotentiary, sent by God, the Sovereign of the universe, to man, the ruler of the earth; he appears officially as representing the Deity; he comes clothed in the power, authority, and sovereignty of God; he is God made manifest in the flesh; his acts are the acts of God, his words are the words of God; his promises and his threats are the promises and threats of God; he that hears him hears God, and he that sees him sees God. If he tells us God is our Father, we know it, we have got beyond belief, we are sure it is so; if he says there is a kingdom of heaven, and an eternal life, we know it is true. If he shows us the way, and points out the path, we know it to be the true way and the right path, because the voice of God has spoken it.

As we have said, the great mission of the Christ was to bring life and immortality to light, and to reveal the being and purposes of God. Who would believe the teachings of an unenlightened man on these subjects? Who could reveal the thoughts, wishes, desires, purposes, of God, except one who had been with God, or who had received divine illumination? The revelations of Jehovah to Moses were made amid the thunder, fire, and smoke of Sinai, in the full sight of the people; but no visible revelation was made to Christ that he should promulgate. We find the Christ claiming pre-existence, that he was taught by God, that he came from God, and that he was sent to accomplish a certain work; that he came not of himself, but that God sent him.

"For I am come down from heaven, not to do mine own will, but the will of him that sent me." (John vi. 38.)

"I came forth and am come from God; for neither have I come of myself, but he sent me." (John viii. 42.)

"I came not to call the righteous, but sinners." (Matt. ix. 13.)

"Think not that I came to send peace on the earth. I came not to send peace, but a sword." (Matt. x. 34.)

"For the Son of man is come to seek and to save that which was lost." (Luke xix. 10.)

"He that cometh from heaven is above all. What he hath seen and heard, of that he beareth witness."

"I know whence I came, and whither I go." (John viii. 14.)

"I am not alone, but I and the Father that sent me." (John viii. 16.)

"Ye are of this world. I am not of this world." (John viii. 23.)

"He that sent me is true; and the things which I heard from him, these speak I unto you." (John viii. 26.)

"I do nothing of myself; but as the Father taught me, I speak of these things; and he that sent me is with me." (John viii. 29.)

"I speak the things which I have seen with my Father." (John vii. 38.)

"Verily, verily, I say unto you, Before Abraham was, I am." (John viii. 58.)

"Say ye of him whom the Father sanctified and sent into the world, Thou blasphemest"? (John x. 36.)

"And now, O Father, glorify thou me with thine own self, with the glory which I had with thee before the world was." (John xvii. 5-8.)

"For thou lovedst me before the foundations of the world." (John xvii. 24.)

"I came forth from the Father, and am come into the world. Again, I leave the world, and go to the Father." (John xvi. 28.)

"Jesus saith unto them, I proceeded forth and came from God." (John.)

Apparently Jesus was a frequent visitor to Jerusalem. At these times he probably remained at the house of his disciple John. Here he came in contact with the priests of the temple and the learned men of Jerusalem, with whom he held the conversations detailed by John.

In many of these conversations it is evident that he spoke directly to their belief that the

Messiah must be the Son of Jehovah, and wield his power. He boldly avowed that he was the Son of God; that he came from him, and had been taught by him; that whatever he had seen his Father do, that could he do; that he was endowed with the power and authority of Jehovah; and he referred to his doctrines, his revelations, and his miracles, as evidence of the truth of his claims.

V.

THE FIRST AND SECOND REVELATIONS COMPARED.

WE have claimed that the revelations made through the Christ were in all essential features the same as those given to the Aryas. In this chapter we propose to examine and compare the teachings of the Christ with the religious belief of the Aryas as shown in the allegory.

ONE GOD.

The revelation made to the Aryas commences with the grand declaration, that, "in the beginning *God* created the heaven and the earth." This is followed by the continued and reiterated statement that creation in all its separate parts was the work of his hands; and after the work is completed, and every thing pronounced finished in accordance with the intent and purpose of the Deity, — the earth filled with the flora, fauna, and man suitable to its various parts, — the writer enters into particulars. As if by re-iteration to make certainty doubly sure, he repeats, " The Lord God made the earth and the heavens," and further says, "He *made* every plant of the field *before* it was in the earth, and every herb of the field *before* it grew;" that "out of the ground the Lord God *formed* every beast of the field and every fowl of the air," and that "the Lord God *formed* man of the dust of the ground," also, — thus showing the special and individual formation and creation by God of every living thing.

These statements formed a part of the Jewish scriptures, and were believed by them: consequently the Christ passes over this subject without comment, taking their belief in it for granted, emphasizing its teachings on one point only, in his quotation from the Hebrew Scriptures, "Hear, O Israel: the Lord thy God is *one* Lord."

The Hebrews believed in and had worshipped many gods. Their faith in the gods of Egypt in the time of Moses had been so strong, that only the most stupendous miracles — by which the power of these gods had been set at naught, and the superior power of Jehovah shown — had given them confidence to act under the guidance of Moses, and take the necessary steps for their deliverance. This belief in and worship of other gods is shown throughout their history. They bowed down to the golden calf in Sinai, and to the many gods of the Canaanites. Elijah at one time supposed that he was the sole worshipper of Jehovah; and, when reproved, the claim is made for only "seven thousand in Israel which have not bowed to Baal," out of its many millions of inhabitants.

Many times and oft they departed from the worship of Jehovah, and offered sacrifice to Baal, Ashtoreth, Molech, Chemosh, and other gods of Moab, Ammon, Syria, Zidon, and Babylonia. They offered their children in sacrifice on the altar to Molech. "Yea, they sacrificed their sons and their daughters unto devils, and shed innocent blood, even the blood of their sons and of their daughters, whom they sacrificed unto the idols of Canaan; and the land was polluted with blood." ... "Wherefore my fury and mine anger was poured forth, and was kindled in the cities of Judah and in the streets of Jerusalem, and they are wasted and desolate, saith the Lord." "All nations shall say, Wherefore hath the Lord done this unto this land? What meaneth the heat of this great anger? Then men shall say, Because they have forsaken the covenant of the Lord God of their fathers, which he made with them when he brought them forth out of the land of Egypt. For they went and served other gods, and worshipped them, gods whom they knew not, and whom he had not given unto them; and the anger of the Lord was kindled against this land, to bring upon it all the curses that are written in this book."

The Jews at the time of Christ still believed in other gods, in the gods of other nations, as did all mankind; but they had learned a lesson in adversity, and they worshipped Jehovah only. The constant fulfilment of the covenant or contract made by their fathers, the blessings bestowed upon their nation when they worshipped him, and the cursings or punishments received when they departed from him, had been so fully shown in their history as prepared (by Nehemiah) for that purpose, that, since their return from captivity, they had been kept in full allegiance to Jehovah. As by contact with other nations they had become more enlightened, their service had become more elaborate in its forms and ceremonies, and its outward observances were more minute and formal, while the thought they represented had been hidden or lost.

The Aryas had believed in a spiritual power, or in spiritual laws beyond, above, and controlling the natural laws, or laws of nature, which spiritual power was placed in the hands of men when they had arrived at their highest spiritual position.

This same power over nature, called in the Hebrew Scriptures the "spirit of God," and, when

God is represented as speaking, "my spirit," and represented as the power, energy, will, and enlightening influence of the Deity, was given in a restricted degree to Moses, to Joshua, and the prophets, that they might carry out the purposes of God.

In the Christian Scriptures it is called the "Holy Ghost," the "Holy Spirit;" it is poured out, it is given, it comes unannounced, it comes from God. Elisabeth, Zacharias, John, were filled with the Holy Ghost; it descends on Jesus of Nazareth in the form of a dove, on the apostles in tongues of flame; it is bestowed by the Christ, and by the apostles, by man on man. In all these cases it is a spiritual influence, enlightenment, and power, bestowed on man.

Neither the Hebrews of old, nor the Jews of the time of the Christ, ever believed in it as a person or as a God. Nowhere does the Christ speak of the Holy Spirit, or Holy Ghost, as a being to be worshipped, or as one part or person of a Godhead: it is always as an influence or power coming from and bestowed by God.

The first commandment promulgated through Moses is, "I am the Lord thy God, which have brought thee out of the land of Egypt, out of the house of bondage. Thou shalt have no other gods before me." In all the Hebrew Scriptures, when the Deity is represented as speaking of himself, and when he is spoken of, there is no instance where more than one God is mentioned.

In the Christian Scriptures, the Christ always speaks of God as one. He never mentions the Holy Ghost as God, and never speaks of himself but as the Son of man or Son of God; and the idea of a plurality of gods, or a triple Godhead, cannot be found in any of his words. God alone is the author and sustainer of all. His sayings are still more forcible when referring to the Father, whom he constantly mentions as the author of all power.

In illustration of our position, we will transcribe a few of the many sayings of Christ, and of the teachings of the apostles : —

"And this is life eternal, that they should know thee, the only true God."

"With God all things are possible." (Matt. xix. 26.)

"God is not the God of the dead, but of the living." (Matt. xxii. 32.)

"That they might know thee the only true God." (John xvii. 3.)

"There is none good but one, that is God." (Matt. xix. 17.)

"Not that any man hath seen the Father, save he which is from God." (John vi. 46.)

"If any man willeth to do his will, he shall

know of the teaching, whether it be of God." (John vii. 17.)

"He that is of God heareth the words of God." (John viii. 47.)

"And the high priest said unto him, I adjure thee by the living God." (Matt. xxvi. 63.)

These are sufficient to show Christ's belief, as well as that of the Jews generally.

The apostles were to preach the doctrines of Christ throughout the world, and examination shows an unanimity of teaching in this respect; they refer every thing to God, as did Christ, and but one God is known to or taught by them. All the apostles speak of God as the power through whom Christ performed his miracles, and who raised him from the dead. Peter says,—

"The God of our fathers hath glorified his servant Jesus." (Acts iii. 13.)

"Jesus of Nazareth, a man approved of God unto you by mighty works and wonders and signs, which God did by him in the midst of you." (Acts ii. 22.)

"This Jesus did God raise up." (Acts ii. 32.)

The writings of Paul are full of expressions of belief in one God:—

"To us there is one God." (1 Cor. viii. 6.)

"One God and Father of all." (Eph. iv. 6.)

"God which raiseth the dead." (2 Cor. i. 9.)

"God, that hath made the world, and all things therein." (Acts xvii. 24.)

"Whether ye eat or drink, or whatever ye do, do all to the glory of God." (1 Cor. x. 31.)

"That your faith should not stand in the wisdom of men, but in the power of God." (1 Cor. ii. 5.)

"Now he that establisheth us with you in Christ, and anointed us, is God." (2 Cor. i. 21.)

"But all things are of God." (1 Cor. xi. 12.)

"Ye are come unto the city of the living God." (Heb. xii. 22.)

"And every tongue shall confess to God." (Rom. xiv. 11.)

"For our God is a consuming fire." (Heb. xii. 29.)

"He that built all things is God." (Heb. iii. 4.)

"But God is one." (Gal. iii. 20.)

"There is none other God but one." (1 Cor. viii. 4.)

"Then cometh the end, when he shall deliver up the kingdom to God." (1 Cor. xv. 24.)

"But to us there is but one God, the Father, of whom are all things." (1 Cor. viii 6.)

These are a few of the expressions of the apostles. They invariably speak of God as one; there is no division or multiplication of being; all their writings show that they believed in the declaration of Moses adopted and indorsed by Christ: "**Hear, O Israel: the Lord thy God is one Lord.**"

THE LOVE OF GOD.

The great evangel has by the providence of God been safely kept until man has reached that point of spiritual intelligence which enables him to grasp and receive the full revelation as delivered originally to the Aryas, supplemented and made complete in the doctrine of the love of God for his human children, as taught by Jesus the Christ.

This love is also taught in the original revelation. The principal object in the creation of the world was the comfort, pleasure, and happiness of man.

As the mother prepares the dainty dresses for her child, or the father provides toys and playthings to give pleasure to his son; as both together labor and strive to prepare him for the situation in life they hope he will fill, so the Deity, with infinite love, filled the earth with blessings for the enjoyment of his children. The beauty of the sky and clouds, of the flowers, fields, and forests; the majesty of the mountains and seas; the herds of animals for his use; the countless fruits to please his taste; the whole boundless universe in all its sublimity and loveliness, — all speak of the love of an affectionate Father.

God is love. He cannot be worshipped in fear; for worship is love and trust expressed in action, and perfect love casteth out fear. Heaven is love, and love is the key of entrance thereto. Love is its language, and the breath of its being; and none but those who love God and their fellow-man can enter therein. Love is the joy of heaven, the happiness of earth, the atmosphere in which we live and move and have our being. Creation is love embodied in acts. This earth is filled with the evidences of the Creator's love for his children. Every thing was created for their convenience and happiness. Every imagination of the heart of man was to be satisfied.

This earth is God's great kindergarten; his infant-school, filled with object-lessons, teaching of his great and constant love for his children, and of his solicitude for their welfare and happiness.

It has been asked, Why did God cause his children, the objects of this great love, to be born on the earth? Would it not have been much better for them to have been born in heaven, where their innocence would be unsullied by sin, where there was no temptation to wrong? Why did God place them in the midst of sin and want and crime and misery?

Love is again the answer. Where, otherwise, would be the love of parents for their children, of children for their parents, of brother and sister, of youth and maiden, of husband and wife, and of man for man? God sought to give to man some of the happiness he himself enjoyed.

Love created temptation, that through the overcoming of temptation man might obtain virtue. Virtue is personified in the Christ; innocence, in the child in his arms. The one has experienced temptation, trial, suffering, and in the conflict has become a higher, stronger, fuller, more complete man, his spiritual faculties alive, awake, and earnest: the other is placid, calm, without power or force of character, simply existing.

God has placed us here to try our spiritual strength, with the result that he who overcomes becomes indeed a glorious son of God.

This world is no place of probation: it is a place of growth; a place in which to learn of God, of his love and care, and of his requirements; a place in which to study the manners, customs, habits, and language of heaven; to put in practice that love for God and man which is in its atmosphere, and controls its being.

God does not create sin. He did create the animal instincts, which he pronounced good for the animal man: but when man's intellect had advanced so far as to obtain a knowledge of God and of his laws and requirements, the instincts ceased to be a guide to man; the laws of God overruled and controlled them, and placed them in subjection. These instincts then became tempters, and urged man to submit to their control. If man succumbs to their temptations, he reduces himself to the position of the animal, and partakes of their nature to the extent of his fall. If he resists and overcomes the temptations, he is spiritually advanced to the extent of the power of the temptation, and the determination and force requisite to overcome it.

Man is tempted to sin, not by God, but by the instincts of his animal nature. In overcoming these temptations to wrong-doing, his highest spiritual powers are brought into active exertion; by this means they are strengthened and enlarged. Besides this, all the best impulses of our being are excited by our surroundings. Love for the sinner brings out our self-sacrifice, disinterestedness, generosity, charity, devotedness, unselfishness, manliness; while the sinner may learn repentance and humility, and the suffering learn patience, fortitude, gratitude, love. All the virtues are brought out by contact with temptation, poverty, sickness, sin, and crime, — virtues which do not belong to, and cannot be called into being by, innocence.

Temptation is a God-sent boon to man; given him in love, to make him a firmer, stronger, and more powerful spiritual being.

There is no hell except in the heart of the wicked, and God has created no devil to torment his children. He who in fear of the devil hastens to save his life, will lose it; because the action is selfish, and the selfish man cannot enter heaven.

Here man commences his eternal existence, lays the foundation of love to God and love to man, and of knowledge in intellectual and spiritual things, which shall be of advantage to him in the life beyond. Here he weakens or strengthens his character by contact with temptation; and, as he overcomes, approaches nearer and nearer to him who is our exemplar, the perfect man; to him who received the expressed approbation of God, in the words, "This is my beloved Son, in whom I am well pleased: hear ye him."

God has placed man on this earth in situations to bring out all his intellectual and spiritual powers; all the wisdom which he obtains here will help him in the world beyond.

Man is entitled to his whole life here, his three-score years and ten. It is for his good, his spiritual welfare, that he should fill out his term.

Every one whose life is shortened by sin, disease, or accident, is deprived of just so much of necessary development; and it is the duty of every one to care for this life as not abusing it, and to seize every opportunity for intellectual and spiritual advance, while he especially cultivates in his heart love to God and love to man, and uses the powers and blessings God has given him for the benefit of his brothers and sisters in God.

Every child who dies is by that means deprived of that spiritual energy developed by contact with and resistance of temptation, which gives strength of character and determination of purpose. He may be comparatively innocent, but that does not compensate for the loss or want of virtue. He loses also his intellectual and spiritual initiation, and, above all, the opportunity to cultivate his love to God by doing good to his fellow-man.

In the difference between virtue and innocence, as depicted above, we can see one reason why God placed man on this earth subject to temptation and trial. Man is born an innocent being, subject to the laws of his being as an animal. He becomes an intellectual, and finally a spiritual, being. Each of these steps in advance brings corresponding duties, and subjects him to the new laws of his advance. As the intellectual position of a Bacon or a Newton, the spirituality of a St. John or a Channing, is more to be desired than the ignorance of the babe, so the virtue of a Christ, obtained by resisting temptation and overcoming evil, is more to be desired than the innocence of the same infant.

THE KINGDOM OF HEAVEN.

In the allegory, the Aryas, previous to partaking of the fruit of the tree of knowledge, were governed by the law of man commonly called the moral law, the law of right and wrong, of mine and thine. This is the foundation of all governments, and is found in all religious codes. But the law and requirements of God were unknown.

The first movement toward a spiritual life is the recognition of the being of God, and a knowledge of his requirements. Under the symbol of partaking of the fruit of the tree of the knowledge of good and evil, the Aryas, it is recorded, obtained this higher, this spiritual, knowledge.

The Christ's first cry was, "The kingdom of heaven is at hand." His second was, "Now the kingdom of God is preached unto you."

The knowledge of good and evil revealed to the Aryas the tree of life; and through their knowledge of the laws and requirements of the Deity, they learned how they might obtain eternal life.

So the Christ revealed to man the being of God, his laws and requirements, and showed unto them eternal life, and the way whereby it may be obtained.

The Aryas were governed by their laws of right and wrong, and were innocent of evil until they obtained the knowledge of good and evil; so the Christ says to the Jews, You were governed by and judged by the laws of Moses until John, you knew no higher law; since which time the kingdom of heaven is preached unto you. The being, law, and government of God are now taught you, and from this time you will be governed and judged by these laws. As was the case in the allegory, the laws of the kingdom of heaven go beyond the knowledge of right and wrong as between man and man, and reach the springs of action in the heart.

The kingdom of heaven is within you, says the Christ, your rule of life and spring of action; its laws are laws of righteousness or right doing; they lead to the carrying-out, the doing, of the will of God, as expressed in the universal law of love and shown in the life of Christ.

"Seek ye *first* the kingdom of heaven," is the Christ's call. He likens this knowledge to a pearl of great price, whose value is beyond riches; to a treasure hid in the field, for which a man will give all that he hath. Its influence on the man who obeys the laws of the kingdom is like leaven; it changes and sweetens his whole character, and he becomes a new man. As the grain of mustard-seed in the soil, so he grows in all goodness until the birds of the air rest in its branches; that is, all who need come to him for aid and comfort.

All are called, but many seek to come without obeying the laws of the kingdom; like the tares in the wheat, in the day of trial they fail and are cast out. He who came to the wedding-feast without the proper garment, that is, without proper preparation; and the foolish virgins who allowed their lamps to go out, that is, did not continue in the right, — are expelled and shut out of the kingdom. All must work in God's vineyard, each according to his talents and opportunities; those who do not will be thrust out of the kingdom. The earnest worker, whether for one hour or twelve, will receive the "Well done, good and faithful servant; enter thou into the joy of thy Lord."

Christ proclaimed the kingdom of heaven, and immediately published the laws of that kingdom. These laws were to govern the actions of men upon the earth. Those who do the will of God as therein required are the children of the kingdom. They have already become members of the kingdom by subjecting themselves to its laws, and obeying the will of its ruler, God.

Something more than mere intellectual belief in this doctrine is required. Only those who *do* the will of God as expressed in those laws will be received into the kingdom. Heaven is a state of existence, both here and hereafter. No one enters who does not strongly desire and earnestly strive for it.

Heaven being a state of existence, commenced on this earth but continuing beyond, the entrance to which is obtained here; let us study carefully the conditions of entrance as given us by the Christ, the only being authorized by God to teach us. He says, —

"Not every one that saith unto me, Lord, Lord, shall enter into the kingdom of heaven; but he that doeth the will of my Father which is in heaven." (Matt. vii. 21.)

It is not necessary that we should know that such a being as the Christ ever existed, to enter into heaven. Doing the will of God gives us the entrance thereto. Abraham, Isaac, and Jacob had no knowledge of the Christ: yet they were admitted into heaven, because they lived up to the light which they had received, poor and crude as was their knowledge of God, and reprehensible as were many of their actions, judged in the light of Christianity. They were models for their time, and received their reward.

The Christ enunciates as the sum and substance of the requirements of God: "Thou shalt love the Lord thy God with all thy heart, and with all thy soul, and with all thy mind, and with all thy strength."

"With all thy heart," that is, with all the affections; "with all thy soul," is all thy religious and emotional nature; "with all thy mind," that is, with all the brightness and vigor of thine intellect; and "with all thy strength," is with all the power and force of thy nature. Not a passive love, but an active, energetic, aggressive, and glowing love, showing itself in all your life and actions, and causing you to use all the powers he has given you in his service. To this he adds, "Thou shalt love thy neighbor as thyself." And his comment upon them is, "There is none other commandment greater than these."

In these commandments, known to the Jews, but until then unnoticed, the Christ proclaimed in a condensed form the laws governing the kingdom of God. Love, and love alone, is the key which unlocks the gates of heaven.

"Among them that are born of woman, there hath not arisen a greater than John the Baptist: yet he that is but little in the kingdom of heaven is greater than he." (Matt. xi. 11.) Although he prophesied that it was at hand, he knew not what it was.

"The law and the prophets were until John. From that time the gospel of the kingdom of God is preached." (Luke xvi. 16.)

"The kingdom of God cometh not with observation; neither shall they say, Lo, here! or Lo, there! For, behold, the kingdom of God is within you." (Luke xvii. 20, 21.)

"Except ye be born anew, ye cannot see the kingdom of God." (John iii. 3.)

"Seek ye first the kingdom of God, and his righteousness." (Matt. vi. 3.)

"Suffer the little children to come unto me, for of such is the kingdom of God." (Mark x. 16.)

"Blessed are ye poor, for yours is the kingdom of God." (Mark vi. 20.)

"There be some of them that stand here, which shall in no wise taste of death, till they see the kingdom of God." (Mark ix. 27.)

"How hardly shall they that have riches enter into the kingdom of God!" (Mark x. 21.)

"Whosoever, therefore, shall break one of these commandments, and shall teach men so, shall be called least in the kingdom of heaven; but whosoever shall do and teach them, he shall be called great in the kingdom of heaven." (Matt. v. 19.)

"And Philip preached the good tidings concerning the kingdom of God." (Acts viii. 12.)

"That through many tribulations we must enter into the kingdom of God." (Acts xiv. 27.)

"Be it known therefore unto you, that this salvation of God is sent unto the Gentiles; they will also hear." (Acts xxviii. 28.)

"For the kingdom of God is not eating and drinking, but righteousness, and peace, and joy in the Holy Ghost." (Rom. xiv. 17.)

"For the kingdom of God is not in word, but in power." (1 Cor. iv. 21.)

GOD OUR FATHER.

The fatherhood of God and the sonship of man, which was emphatically declared by the Aryas, was also taught by the Christ, though not so fully as in the original revelation. The Christ was prevented by the spiritual ignorance of the Jews from proclaiming it broadly; but in connection with himself, and his position as Son of God and Son of man, he continually asserts the same position for all mankind. This teaching was not received by the Jews pleasantly. They called it blasphemy, and attempted to stone the Christ for its utterance.

Even to this time it has been received by Christians only in a vague, uncertain sense. Acknowledged by the intellect, it has not pierced the heart.

Within a few years only has it been accepted by a few as an actual fact, and man realized that he is a son of God, partaking of his nature, — a brother of the Christ in both his divine and human nature.

In our former volume we showed that man is an actual son of God, — that God, by a special act of his Spirit, becomes the father of every human being; that he selected the woman as his procreative agent, through whom his spiritual children are brought into being.

The fatherhood of God and the sonship of man, as declared by Christ, was a doctrine not only entirely new to the Jews, but to all mankind. The Jews were proud of their descent from Abraham; but to claim to be a son of Jehovah was in their eyes sacrilege, and in the case of Christ they resented it by death.

"Our Father who art in heaven," is the declaration of Christ; not his Father alone, but *our* Father, the Father of all mankind. He repeatedly gives utterance to the same thought: —

"Be ye therefore perfect, as your heavenly Father is perfect." (Matt. v. 29.)

"Else ye have no reward with your Father which is in heaven." (Matt. vi. 1.)

"And thy Father which seeth in secret shall recompense thee." (Matt. vi. 4.)

"Pray to thy Father which is in secret, and thy Father which seeth in secret shall recompense thee." (Matt. vi. 6.)

"For your Father knoweth what things ye have need of." (Matt. vi. 8.)

"For if ye forgive men their trespasses, your heavenly Father will also forgive you." (Matt. vi. 14.)

"That ye may be sons of your Father which is in heaven." (Matt. v. 45.)

"Be ye merciful, even as your Father is merciful." (Luke xliv. 36.)

"Even so it is not the will of your Father which is in heaven, that one of these little ones should perish." (Matt. xviii. 14.)

"I ascend unto my Father and your Father, and my God and your God." (John xx. 17.)

The apostles teach the same doctrine: —

"For ye are all sons of God." (Gal. iii. 26.)

"In this the children of God are manifest." (1 John iii. 10.)

"The Spirit himself beareth witness with our spirits, that we are the children of God; and if children, then heirs; heirs of God, and joint heirs with Christ." (Rom. viii. 16, 17.)

"Then shall they be called sons of the living God." (Rom. x. 26.)

"And because ye are sons, God hath sent forth the spirit of his own Son into your hearts."

Nominally mankind have accepted Christ's teaching that they are children of God, — his sons and his daughters, — and in their prayers they address God as "our Father which art in heaven;" but they seem to accept and believe it in any but a real sense. They do not seem to realize the fact that they are actually the children of the most high God; that they are each and all known to him, and loved and cared for individually by him; that they are sons of God in the same way, to the same extent, and with the same being, as Jesus the Christ was Son of God.

Men, in their spiritual ignorance, do not yet understand what it means to be a son of God; they do not realize that they partake of the nature of the Deity in the same way that as son of man they partake of the human nature.

When God says, "Let us make man in our image," we should remember that God speaks not at all, but that it is the author placing the words in the mouth of God, as a statement of his own belief or knowledge. This statement is confirmed by the Christ, who tells us that God is our Father, and that we are his children. A child partakes of the nature of his father, and man himself proves that he is the son of God by wielding the powers of the Deity.

Man is a creator, not only of inanimate objects of wood, clay, stone, metals, and animal and vegetable substances, but he also creates new varieties of plants, flowers, fruits, and grains, improved varieties of the horse, ox, sheep, swine, dog, and other animals, to suit his taste, convenience, or necessity. He is omnipotent over the brute creation, and causes many of the powers of nature to obey his will. He is largely omniscient and omnipresent, causing the lightning to bear his messages across sea and land, and inform him of the daily occurrences in the furthermost parts of the earth. Creator, omnipotent, omniscient, and omnipresent in his finite sphere, he exhibits his likeness to his infinite Father, God. He is doing this now in his childhood of existence, is gradually obtaining power over the works of his Father's hands, and causing them to obey his will. If he now, in his spiritual infancy, exerts so much power, what may we not expect from him as he rises nearer and nearer to the likeness of the perfect man in Christ Jesus? May we not believe, as man's life spiritually approaches that of the Christ, that the power over nature which he possessed by reason of his singleness of purpose, and pureness of heart, may also be placed in the hands of man, to be used for the relief of pain and sickness, for the restoration of sight to the blind, hearing to the deaf, and a sound body to the paralyzed, lame, and injured?

These are some of the powers of the Deity which man, the son of God, is using, or beginning to use, by reason of his birthright.

Groping in the darkness of spiritual ignorance, he has yet, like a child, grasped some of the powers belonging to his nature, and almost by instinct obtained marvellous results. How much greater and more powerful will they be, when, recognizing his birthright, he seeks the aid of his Father in his endeavor to bless mankind!

But, while man employs these material powers of the Deity, he must remember that he is also possessor of his Father's spiritual nature. Love, mercy, justice, truthfulness, faithfulness, — all of these characteristics of God belong to man as son of God; and he is required to seek for them with all his heart, and use them for the benefit of others. How much greater will be the results when man becomes aware that because he is the son of God he partakes fully of his nature!

The Christ has shown what it is possible for man to do in using the powers of God, and what it is possible for him to be, when, guided and influenced by the characteristics of the Deity, he is in full sympathy with the purposes of his Father in heaven.

The Christ has given us a rule, by following which we shall attain both material and spiritual good in a degree corresponding with our ability and the earnestness of our prayers.

The universal rule is this: —

"Ask, and ye shall receive; seek, and ye shall find; knock, and it shall be opened unto you;" and Christ emphasizes this rule by a double declaration of it, "For every one that asketh receiveth, and he that seeketh findeth, and unto him that knocketh the door shall be opened."

Asking in words is nothing but wind. Desire must develop in action, — in seeking, searching, knocking, working; giving heart, soul, mind, strength, the whole being, to accomplishing the object desired.

A man wishes to obtain riches: he asks for it in act. He rises early, and retires late; he throws into the accomplishing of his desire the time, strength, earnestness, and perseverance of his whole being, and succeeds.

Another asks for knowledge: he studies late and early, gives his whole time and strength to the fulfilment of his purpose, and becomes a learned man.

Others pray for fame, for political position,

military power: each gives his time, talents, earnestness, to attain his object; and his success is in just proportion to his ability, and the earnestness of his work.

So, in the higher spiritual wants, make your prayer active; let your desires be accompanied by action, seeking and working until the door is found, and by that knocking which shall open the door of success, and you enter into the realization of your spiritual desires. The whole material and spiritual universe will be opened to the sons of God who shall earnestly desire to enter.

ETERNAL LIFE THE GIFT OF GOD.

A future life was revealed to the Aryas, which should be theirs on complying with the conditions. The fruit of the tree of life could not be stolen or obtained surreptitiously. The tree was protected from man by the flaming sword of God's requirements. Man was created with the ability to desire, receive, and enjoy it; but only by doing the will of God could he obtain the coveted prize. It was in the hands of the Deity alone, for him to give in accordance with his will and promise.

The Christ taught the same doctrine. Eternal life was in the hands of God. He had promised it as a gift to all who should do his will. The Christ revealed what were the requirements, in what way man could obtain this great boon. No other religious teacher has revealed either the life or the way.

He lived the life, and showed the way. He was the way, the truth, the life. He was the light of men: without him, they groped in darkness. His teachings were springs of living water, his truths meat and drink to the soul. His death and resurrection opened the door. He was the resurrection and the life. Thus, in this literal manner, in his life, death, and resurrection, he embodied all his teachings.

"He that heareth my word, and believeth him that sent me, *hath eternal life, and cometh not into judgment, but hath passed out of death into life.*" (John v. 24.) He has not to wait until death shall open his eyes, and bring him into judgment; but he hath already passed through the judgment, already come into the kingdom of heaven, already hath obtained and doth enjoy the gift of God, — eternal life.

"And this is life eternal, that they should know thee, the only true God, and him whom thou didst send, even Jesus Christ." (John xvii. 3.)

"He whom God hath sent speaketh the words of God; for he giveth not the Spirit by measure. The Father loveth the Son, and hath given all things into his hands. He that believeth on the

Son *hath* eternal life; he that obeyeth not the Son shall not see life." (John iii. 34–36.)

The Christ likens his teachings to "water, springing up into everlasting life." He says, "I am the bread of life which came down from heaven, that a man may eat thereof, and never die." He tells men to "work for the meat which abideth unto eternal life."

Although the Christ taught that "he that believeth on the Son hath eternal life," it is evident that more than intellectual belief is required. He continues, "He that *obeyeth* not the Son shall not see life."

The Christ requires us to assimilate his teachings, as the body assimilates food. His teachings must be like water, like bread, like meat, taken into the system, sustaining the life, giving power and strength. We must live his teachings as he did, if we would obtain eternal life.

The test of the Christian is the fruit. "Every good tree bringeth forth good fruit: therefore, by their fruits shall ye know them." The fig-tree that was green and flourishing, but bore no fruit, he condemned.

The Christ says, "Not every one that saith unto me, Lord, Lord, shall enter into the kingdom of heaven; but he that *doeth the will* of my Father which is in heaven." There is no shibboleth in the mere name of Christ to save men. Intellectual belief in creeds formed by man will not give entrance into eternal life. The life is the test, and the only test. Good fruit is the requirement of Christ. Only "he that doeth the will of my Father which is in heaven" will be admitted.

"Many will say to me in that day, Lord, Lord, did we not prophesy in thy name, and by thy name cast out devils, and by thy name do many wonderful works? And then will I profess unto them, I never knew you: depart from me, ye workers of iniquity." And he likens those who hear his words, and *do them*, to wise men who build upon a rock; and those who hear, and *do them not*, to foolish men who build upon the sand.

Christ, after his interview with the young man that had great possessions, says, "It is hard for a rich man to enter into the kingdom of heaven;" and again, "I say unto you, It is easier for a camel to go through a needle's eye, than for a rich man to enter into the kingdom of heaven. And when the disciples heard it, they were astonished exceedingly, saying, Who then can be saved? And Jesus, looking upon them, said to them, With man this is impossible: but with God all things are possible."

In the parable of the talents, Christ reveals

why it is so difficult for a rich man to enter the kingdom of God.

Every man has one or more talents, that is, means and opportunities of doing good. God has given to some learning, others power, to others riches, and in that way multiplied their opportunities to do good, and in the same way multiplied their obligations. The poorest may give a cheering word, a helping hand, a cup of cold water, may visit and comfort the sick, may give a crust to a starving man, may warm a freezing one, and receive the acknowledgment of Christ, "Inasmuch as ye did it unto one of these least, ye have done it unto me." In a thousand ways, the poorest may show their love for others, and thus use the single talent God has intrusted to them.

Others by reason of position, learning, power, riches, have multiplied opportunities for good; and with them come multiplied obligations. They are so many talents placed in their hands by God for use, not for their own selfish aggrandizement or pleasure, but to bless others; and they are called upon by Christ to use them for the purposes required of them. "To whomsoever much is given, of him shall much be required: and to whom they commit much, of him will they ask the more." With so much greater means of usefulness, their obligations are just so much greater: he who has the trust, must seek opportunities to fulfil it. He that uses his talents for his own pleasure only, buries his Lord's money. He does no good to his fellow-creatures, and receives the condemnation, "Inasmuch as ye did it not unto one of these least, ye did it not unto me."

When we see the immense riches placed in the hands of some men, we tremble at the weight of obligation resting upon them. God claims the riches of the earth as belonging to him. Whoever receives them, receives them as the steward of God; and he is required to use them for God's purposes, and to benefit his fellow-man. God requires the interest of his money; and if the possessor neglects to pay it, he receives the condemnation of the wicked and slothful servant.

God requires of man his whole heart, its love, its fervor, its intellect and strength. While he is required to work on this earth to support himself, and those dependent on him, he is also required to do all his work in the spirit of his Master, all being made subsidiary to the grand object of this life, namely, eternal life.

In the endeavor to heap up riches upon this earth, man is apt to give his whole heart to that one object, leaving God's claim entirely out of his thoughts. The law of Christ, "Ask, and ye shall receive; seek, and ye shall find; knock, and it shall be opened unto you," is a law of earth as well as of heaven. Whatever we seek with our whole heart, that we shall obtain. Whether it be " the kingdom of God, and his righteousness," or wisdom, glory, riches, whatever it may be, we shall obtain it to a greater or less degree according to our ability. All of these talents bear corresponding obligations; and woe to him who does not fulfil the obligations resting upon him, and use them for the benefit of his fellow-man! The requirements of God are so great and so strict, that we can readily see why it is so hard, and almost impossible, for a man who puts his trust in riches to enter into heaven.

And the witness is this, that God *gave* unto us eternal life, and this life is in his Son. He that hath the Son hath the life. (1 John v. 11, 12.)

Christ shows that those who do the will of God as little children will receive eternal life; that those who show a loving and forgiving disposition, will themselves receive forgiveness; that if the rich man uses the riches placed in his hands as a sacred trust to be accounted for, then he will receive eternal life.

God requires all men to *work* in his vineyard. Those that heed the call will meet their reward. There can be no lazy Christian: every man is called upon to work. Whoever would be first in the kingdom must serve, must work, even as Christ came to work, and even to give his life, that men might know how to obtain eternal life.

In the parable of the householder, he proclaims that the kingdom of God shall be given to those bringing forth the fruits thereof.

In the parable of the talents, it is those who use the talents which God has given them, that receive the commendation of their Lord, and are rewarded.

God calls you to work in his vineyard, to use the talents he has given in doing good, and in advancing his kingdom in the hearts of men. As ye do this, ye will receive the blessing, "Well done, good and faithful servant." And ye shall be your own judges. Every one knows whether, and how earnestly, he is working in the vineyard. If ye are feeding the hungry, clothing the naked, visiting the sick, relieving the distressed, and doing this because you love your fellow-man, then to you is addressed the blessing, "Inasmuch as ye have done it unto one of these my brethren, ye have done it unto me. Come, ye blessed of my Father, inherit the kingdom prepared for you from the foundation of the earth."

Later, he shows that Abraham, Isaac, and Jacob are all members of the kingdom. How? They neither knew of the laws of Moses, nor of Christ.

The Christian Scriptures say of Abraham, that "he wavered not through unbelief, but waxed strong through faith, giving glory to God, and being fully assured that what he had promised he was able also to perform. Wherefore, also, *it was reckoned unto him* for righteousness," or right doing. In other words, Abraham, Isaac, and Jacob lived up to the light which they had, — a very dim and unsatisfactory light, but by keeping faith in God as they knew him, and doing his will so far as it was revealed to them, they were accepted as righteous.

So, too, Moses, Elias, and David are represented as receiving the approval of God; not that they lived perfect lives, but they lived up to the light which they had, or, like David, repented of grievous sins, and were received into life.

Man, while born with the germ of eternal life, can by his own actions kill that germ. Sin is a disease, a poison, which indulged in will kill it. (Luke xx. 25.) "The wages [or result] of sin is death; but the free *gift* of God is eternal life in Christ Jesus our Lord." (Rom. vi. 23.)

"If thou knewest the *gift* of God, and who it is that saith to thee, Give me to drink; thou wouldst have asked of him, and he would have given thee living water. Whosoever drinketh of the water that I shall give him, shall never thirst;

but the water that I shall give him shall become in him a well of water, springing up into eternal life." (John iv. 10-14.)

"Work not for the meat which perisheth, but for the meat which abideth unto eternal life, which the Son of man shall *give* unto you; for him the Father, even God, hath sealed." (John vi. 27-29.)

"*I give* unto them eternal life, and they shall never perish; and no one shall snatch them out of my hand. My Father which hath given them unto me is greater than all, and no one is able to snatch them out of the Father's hand." (John x. 28, 29.)

"These things spake Jesus: and lifting up his eyes to heaven he said, Father, the hour is come; glorify thy Son, that the Son may glorify thee; even as thou gavest him authority over all flesh, that whatsoever thou hast given him, to them he should *give* eternal life. And this is life eternal, that they should know thee the only true God, and him whom thou didst send, even Jesus Christ." (John xvii. 1-3.)

We have said that an actual knowledge of the Christ was not necessary to obtain eternal life. We give some illustrations of this position:—

"And behold, a certain lawyer stood up and tempted him, saying, Master, what shall I do to inherit eternal life? And he said unto him, What is written in the law? How readest thou? And he answering said, Thou shalt love the Lord thy God with all thy heart, and with all thy soul, and with all thy strength, and with all thy mind; and thy neighbor as thyself. And he said unto him, Thou hast answered right. *This do*, and thou *shalt live.*" (Luke x. 25-28.)

That there may be no misunderstanding of his teaching on this point, the Christ, in his parable representing that day which shall come to all, when the secrets of all hearts shall be opened, and the laws of the kingdom applied and enforced, says to those who had loved their fellow-men, and had done good to them, though they knew not that they were thus doing in accordance to the Christ's injunctions, "Come, ye blessed of my Father, inherit the kingdom prepared for you from the foundation of the world; for I was a hungered, and ye gave me meat; I was thirsty, and ye gave me drink; I was a stranger, and ye took me in; naked, and ye clothed me; I was sick, and ye visited me; I was in prison, and ye came unto me." And upon their expressing astonishment, not having known him, he says, "Inasmuch as ye have done it unto one of the least of these my brethren, ye have done it unto me." He says to those who had neglected their duty, who had not loved and aided their fellow-men, "Inasmuch as ye did it not to one of the least of these, ye did it not to me. And these shall go away into everlasting punishment; but the righteous, into life eternal." (Matt. xxv. 31.)

There is here no question of faith, or belief in Christ, in unity or trinity, in Adam's sin or total depravity; but, what have you done to benefit your fellow-men? Love to man is the key to heaven and to eternal life.

Peter teaches the same doctrine: —

"Of a truth, I perceive that God is no respecter of persons; but in every nation he that feareth him, and worketh righteousness, is accepted with him."

It is true, however, that we can *seek* eternal life only through the Christ, for through his teachings only do we know how to obtain it. No other teacher before or since has shown man the way to eternal life. Other foundation can no man lay than that is laid, Jesus Christ.

GOD'S PLAN OF SALVATION.

In the revelation to the Aryas, we find the record that God gave unto man the animal instincts for his rule of life; these were his laws of action, under the guidance of which all his actions were innocent. When these had been enlarged by his intellect, he was governed and judged by the moral law of right and wrong. Not until he had obtained a knowledge of God and of his laws, had partaken of the fruit of the tree of the knowledge of good and evil, was he subject to the higher law of the kingdom of God.

The Christ was prevented by the spiritual ignorance of his time from teaching the same doctrine direct: it would have been misunderstood; but for the instruction of later times, he has given us in three beautiful parables, — which are one, — a clear statement of God's watchfulness and care of his children.

The circumstances under which these parables were uttered are given as follows : —

"Now all the *publicans* and *sinners* were drawing near unto him for to hear him; and both the Pharisees and the scribes murmured, saying, This man receiveth *sinners*, and eateth with them."

In answer to the murmurings of these self-righteous Jews, Christ spoke unto them this parable, saying, —

"What man of you, having a hundred sheep, and having lost one of them, doth not leave the ninety and nine in the wilderness, and go after that which is lost until he find it? And when he hath found it he layeth it on his shoulders rejoicing; and when he cometh home he calleth together his friends and his neighbors, saying unto them, Rejoice with me, for I have found my sheep which was lost. I say unto you, that even so there shall be joy in heaven over one sinner that repenteth, more than over ninety and nine righteous persons which need no repentance."

The civilized nations at the time of the Christ were governed by the moral law of man, the law of right and wrong. They had no knowledge of God or of his laws. They were generally content with merely animal existence. Their lives were spent in animal delights. In the parable, these nations were likened unto sheep; they having as little knowledge of God, as the sheep of its shepherd. As the shepherd searches for the stray sheep, and brings him back to the fold, so God is represented as seeking and caring for his children who in ignorance have wandered away from him; they are his children, he cares for them, and not one is lost.

Christ then utters another parable, enforcing the same lesson respecting another class of individuals and nations, in these words: —

"Or what woman having ten pieces of silver, if she lose one piece, doth not light a lamp, and sweep the house, and seek diligently until she find it? and when she hath found it she calleth together her friends and neighbors, saying, Rejoice with me, for I have found the piece which I had lost. Even so, I say unto you, there is joy in the presence of the angels of God over one sinner that repenteth."

In this parable Christ pictures those individuals and nations who have no knowledge of God, and no law but their instincts, the law of nature. As the money knows not its owner, and rolls away without intent or knowledge, so there are nations who as yet have received no moral light whatever; they have no moral obligations; they are still animals governed by their animal passions and appetites. Yet, as the money belonged to the woman, so these human beings belong to God; they are his children. As the money was stamped with the image and superscription of Cæsar, so these human beings bear God's image and superscription, and are the objects of his love and care. As the woman searched diligently for the lost money, so God watches over and keeps in his own possession these ignorant and darkened children; not one of them is lost, but all are safely kept in his bosom. Or if, in the glimmering of light, one strays away, he is diligently sought, and returned to the care of his owner. Neither of these two classes are sinners, nor are any of them lost.

Having shown to the scribes and Pharisees God's love for the most degraded and ignorant of his children, those whom the Jews held in the utmost scorn and contempt, Christ proceeds to describe still another class of individuals and nations, giving us the well-known parable of the younger son, in which he shows us God's method of proceeding with those who have been brought up in the Father's house, who, like the young man, *wilfully* turn away from the instruction and protection, and break away from the restraints of home, who knowingly depart to revel in sin, even until they become in their desires and inclinations like unto swine. Even they can come back: they are God's children, and he loves and mourns over them. But they are free agents, unlike those described in the first two parables. These are not ignorant of God's laws. They have sinned against light and knowledge, and if they come back it must be of their own free will; they must be ready to acknowledge their sin, and of their own accord seek pardon and forgiveness; they must arise, and go to their Father. Unlike the other cases, God does not personally seek them. They must come to him; they know the way back to his home and his forgiveness. He is ready to meet them while yet a great way off, and he receives them with joy. No long penance, no terrible punishment for what they have done; but they are cleansed and clothed anew, they are met with joy and gladness, and welcomed to the Father's house.

Among the Jews were those who had obtained a partial knowledge of good and evil through the teachings of the prophets and other religious instructors. The scribes and Pharisees, and the more learned of the Jews, were farther advanced in spiritual knowledge than the men of any other nation. They were partially aware of God's requirements, and the Christ designates them as elder sons. This parable, which at the time was directed especially to them, is more particularly applicable to Christians, to whom the Christ has revealed the laws of the kingdom.

Christians, unlike all others, have partaken of the fruit of the tree of the knowledge of good and evil. They are aware of God's laws and requirements. The Christ has placed the laws of the kingdom in their hands; and they, if they stray into evil, can only come back by their own choice, their own free will.

In the parable, the Christ administers a rebuke to the scribes and Pharisees for their selfishness and religious intolerance, which it may be well for men in these days of religious bigotry to remember.

Is it not strange that men calling themselves Christians, and in their acts and lives showing many of the Christian graces, should still, in their spiritual pride, become so stultified and void of true Christian discernment as to claim that God condemns the ignorant millions of men who have not as yet obtained the slightest knowledge of God or of his laws, to endless torment because of their ignorance? God in his original revelation to the Aryas declares that men ignorant of his laws are innocent, not subject to punishment. The Christ in this parable teaches the same great doctrine. Any other course would make God a terrible and bloodthirsty tyrant, such as no words could describe and no imagination of man conceive. The blackest devil that was ever imagined would be an angel of light in comparison.

"And that servant which *knew* his lord's will, and made not ready, nor did according to his will, shall be beaten with *many* stripes; but he that *knew not*, and did things worthy of stripes, shall be beaten with *few* stripes." (Luke xii. 47, 48.)

ETERNAL DEATH, OR DISSOLUTION.

Eternal death, while not distinctly taught to the Aryas, was strongly indicated. Eternal life was the *gift* of God. The tree of life was guarded from all others by the "cherubim and a flaming sword which turned every way, to keep the way of the tree of life." If eternal life was given only to those who do his will, then eternal death must be the fate of all others.

The teachings of Christ show conclusively that there are some who will not obtain eternal life. While he opens the way to immortality, he says that none but those who *do the will* of God will be admitted. The *unforgiving* will not be admitted. "If ye forgive not men their trespasses, neither will your Father forgive your trespasses." In the parable of the householder, he proclaims that the kingdom of God "shall be *taken away*" from those who do not bring forth the fruit thereof.

"*Not* every one that saith unto me, Lord, Lord, shall enter into the kingdom of heaven." (Matt. vii. 21.)

"Strive to enter in at the strait gate; for many, I say unto you, will seek to enter in, and *shall not be able*." (Luke xiii. 24.)

"It is easier for a camel to go through a needle's eye, than for a rich man to *enter into* the kingdom of heaven." (Luke xviii. 25.)

"He that obeyeth not the Son *shall not see life*." (John iii. 36.)

"I have no pleasure in *the death of him that dieth*, saith the Lord God." (Ezek. xviii. 32.)

"If a man see his brother sinning a sin not unto death, he shall ask, and God will give him life for them that sin not unto death. *There is a sin unto death.*" (1 John v. 16.)

"He that hath not the Son of God *hath not life.*" (John v. 12.)

Christ says, "It is not the will of your Father which is in heaven, that one of these little ones *should perish;*" showing that they can perish, that is, cease to exist; not the body, for all perish, but the spiritual being we call soul. Paul says, "For the wages of sin *is death.*" (Rom. vi. 23.) The result or consequences of sin is the death of the sinner. This idea of *destruction* is carried out in all the imagery of the Gospels. Not only is that the case, but the similes used show sudden and immediate destruction in most cases.

Christ says, "Every tree therefore that bringeth not forth good fruit is *hewn down* and cast into the fire." It is burned up, *destroyed*. He says, Christ will "gather his wheat into the garner, but the chaff he will *burn* with unquenchable fire." Nothing will burn and be destroyed quicker than chaff. It is the fire (Christ's words), that is unquenchable. Christ likens those who hear his words, and do them *not*, to a "foolish man which built his house upon the sand," and it fell and was *destroyed*. He tells his disciples, "Be not afraid of them which kill the body, but are not able to *kill the soul;* but rather fear him which is able to *destroy* both *soul* and body in hell;" again indicating the death of the soul. In the parable of the wheat and tares, the tares are gathered into bundles and burned, — *destroyed.*

"Then said Jesus unto his disciples, If any man would come after me, let him deny himself, and take up his cross, and follow me. For whosoever would save his life shall lose it, and whosoever shall lose his life for my sake shall find it. For what shall a man be profited if he shall gain the whole world, and *lose his own soul?*" (Matt. xvi. 24-26.)

In the parable of the wicked husbandmen, he says of their lord: "He will come and *destroy* those wicked men." (Matt. xxi. 41.)

While Christ describes the fate of some as being destroyed suddenly, like chaff and tares burned up in the fire, or like a tree cut down at the roots, others are not destroyed, but are cast out into outer darkness, where shall be weeping and gnashing of teeth, images of sorrow, remorse, despair; still others are represented as receiving eternal punishment.

In the parable of the wedding feast, the servants *cast out* the man without a wedding garment. In the parable of the unfaithful servant, and in the parable of the unprofitable servant, the punishment in each case is the same: "Cast him into outer darkness; there shall be weeping and gnashing of teeth."

"Unto them that obey not the truth, but obey unrighteousness, shall be wrath and indignation, tribulation and anguish, upon every soul of man that worketh evil." (Rom. ii. 8, 9.)

"And one said unto him, Lord, are they few that be saved? And he said unto them, Strive to enter in by the narrow door: for many, I say unto you, shall seek to enter in, and *shall not be able.* When once the master of the house is risen up, and hath shut the door, and ye begin to stand without, and to knock at the door, saying, Lord, open to us; and he shall answer and say to you, I know ye not whence ye are; then shall ye begin to say, We did eat and drink in thy presence, and thou didst teach in our streets. And he shall say, I tell you, I know not whence ye are: depart from me, all ye workers of iniquity. There shall be the weeping and gnashing of teeth."

Two questions arise. Do those who, having committed sin, afterward repent and receive the remission or pardon of their sins, and the gift of eternal life, escape the punishment of their sins? And do those who die unrepentant, and come forth to the resurrection of judgment, have no opportunity in the world beyond to repent of their sins, and by doing works of righteousness there obtain pardon and eternal life?

"The wages," or the result, "of sin is death." Sin produces the death of the spiritual being. As poison or disease in the human frame weakens, paralyzes, and finally destroys the body, so sin, unrepented of, weakens, paralyzes, and finally destroys the soul. The disease may be slight or serious, and be longer or shorter in its action: the result is certain unless arrested in its progress. Christ is the physician who shows us the remedy, and offers us the means of recovery. If we accept his aid, follow his advice, and use the means he offers, we recover, the sickness is overcome, the poison removed, health returns, and eternal life is the result.

But has this poison, this sickness, left no results? As the human frame is weakened by sickness, scarred by wounds, so the spiritual body must bear the effects of sin. God forgives the sins committed against him, and wipes them from the book of *his* remembrance, and grants the repentant sinner eternal life; but can the man forgive himself? Every sin is committed against some other beside God, and bears results that are, perhaps, never-ending. All sins injure others.

The spiritual being who enters into life pardoned by God, has passed through the judgment, condemned not by God nor Christ, but by himself. He sees the long train of evils produced by his own sins, and is anxious to stop their effect, to wipe them out, or do something whereby he may cover them. If he cannot do this, do not his sins pursue and punish him, notwithstanding his pardon? and would not the punishment be increasing and eternal? He must, for his own happiness, cover them over by good deeds; and he must have the opportunity to do this in the world beyond.

These same questions arise with regard to the unrepentant sinner. One man sins. By the mercy of God he is awakened to a sense of his sin, to a judgment here before the resurrection: he repents, his sins are remitted, and he receives the gift of eternal life. Another sins, no worse than the first, is suddenly cut off by death without repentance, and awakes to the resurrection of judgment. Like the first man, is there no opportunity for him to repent of the sins done in the body? Can he not, in his new state of existence, repent, and do something to wipe out or cover his sins? One man is killed by another. The murderer repents of his evil deeds, passes through the judgment here, his sins are remitted, and he enters into life. The victim enters the judgment of the resurrection. Shall he have no opportunity of reform, no opportunity by good works to cover his sins? The death of the mortal body makes no change in the man. What he was before he dropped the earthly clothing, he is afterward, with the same propensities, desires, habits of thought, the love for the same objects. The man whose thoughts rest principally upon "what shall I eat, and what shall I drink, and wherewithal shall I be clothed?" will have the same thoughts beyond, without the power of supplying his desires. He who is immersed in his business will be held down to earth, and still interested in its details, without the ability to take part therein. The man who has made gold his god, and has spent his life in accumulating riches, will still gloat over the gold he sees others spend with such recklessness. "Where your treasure is, there shall your heart be also," is a law of God; and men build here their own prisons, block out their own position hereafter; and the god they worshipped here, they will continue to worship there, unless, awakened to judgment, they repent, and receive the remission of their sins. Men of vicious habits, intemperate, quarrelling, lascivious, murderous, enter the resurrection the same men. All are bound down to earth, some in sorrow, some in shame and despair, some in anger. But God is merciful, and the poison of sin will soon carry off those who do not repent. And again comes the question, Can they repent, and be forgiven?

Christ says, "My Father *worketh* hitherto, and

I work." Work is the necessity of man's nature here, and undoubtedly the law holds good in the future state of existence. Look at the universe, and see God's work; and shall man, who partakes of his nature and being, in the eternal life remain idle? It is impossible. Man has his work to perform in the immortal as in the mortal life. And what should that work be, but the endeavor to benefit the loved whom he has left behind, to wipe out if possible the results of his own sins, or to cover them by good deeds? "He who converteth a sinner from the error of his way *shall save a soul from death*, and shall *cover* a multitude of sins." And shall this be the case only in this world? Can we believe that the departed are unable to influence those whom they have left behind? or have they no ability to benefit others in the other world?

"The Lord is longsuffering to us-ward, not willing that any should perish, but that all should come to repentance." "I have no pleasure in the death of him that dieth, saith the Lord God: wherefore turn yourselves, and live ye." "Even so it is not the will of your Father which is in heaven, that one of these little ones should perish." Then is there no way by which the sinner may even then return to God his Father, and receiving his pardon join the throngs of the blessed?

With our limited vision, if there is no opportunity beyond this little human life, for God's children to come unto him, there seems to be an injustice not in accordance with either his justice, his love, or his desire that all should be saved.

Let us take the instance of the rich young man, of whom it is said, "And Jesus looking upon him *loved him*, and said unto him, One thing thou lackest. Go, sell whatsoever thou hast, and give to the poor, and thou shalt have treasure in heaven; and come, follow me. But his countenance fell at the saying, and he went away sorrowing: for he was one that had great possessions." Here was a man who could say of himself, in reference to the commandments, "All these things have I observed from my youth." Who of us can say the same? And yet he is condemned. Why? Because, having the opportunity, by reason of his great wealth, to do so much good, he had neglected his opportunities, allowed his Lord's money to lie idle; had hid the talents placed in his charge. His possessions belonged to God; he was God's steward, and should have used his Lord's money to aid the distressed. This he had not done: he only thought of himself, used the money for his own pleasure and aggrandizement, and left his brothers in want. And he meets with the condemnation of the servant who had neglected his one talent; namely, to outer darkness.

Is there no opportunity for the man, when he awakes into the resurrection of judgment, to reform, — to repent? Christ says there is a possibility. His disciples ask in wonder, "Who then can be saved?" and his answer is, "With God all things are possible."

In awakening in the outer darkness to a knowledge of our sins, are the tears of remorse and repentance to be of no avail in the other world? In the parable of the unforgiving steward, Christ says, "And his lord was wroth, and delivered him to the tormentors *till he should pay all that was due.*" Here is an indication that after judgment, and the delivery to the tormentors (his own conscience), after the spiritual being awakens to the knowledge of its sins which the resurrection gives, and which is the judgment, even then there is a way left by which payment may be made, by which the sins unrepented of in this life may still be repented of in the other world, and by work and personal exertion the sinner receive pardon and eternal life.

Christ says, "Verily, verily, I say unto you, The hour cometh, and now is, when the *dead* shall hear the voice of the Son of God, and they that hear shall live. . . . For the hour cometh, in which all that are in the tombs shall *hear* his voice, and shall come forth; they that have *done good*, unto the resurrection of life [no creed, or belief in Christ, no profession of faith required, but those that have *done good*]; and they that have done evil, unto the resurrection of judgment." (John v. 19–29.)

What is the resurrection of judgment, but the awakening of conscience?

"For this cause was the gospel preached also to them that are *dead;* that *they* might be judged according to men in the flesh, but *live* according to God in the spirit." (1 Pet. iv. 6.)

In this life, those who have entered into heaven, and have received the gift of eternal life, have passed through the judgment, before the resurrection, and at the death of the body pass from heaven here to heaven above. Those who have not gone through this experience of judgment in this world, pass through the same judgment at their resurrection. May not the sinner who awakens to a knowledge of his sins at his resurrection, be able to repent and do works of righteousness, even as is required of those who repent here, and there receive the forgiveness of God? "If a man see his brother sinning a sin not unto death, *he shall ask*, and *God will give him* life for them that sin not unto death." And if prayers for those whom we love are answered here, is there no hope that prayers for those who have gone before may be equally as effectual with God?

God is love; and he loves the children he has made, and is not willing that the least of us should perish, but that all should receive eternal life. He rejoices more over one sinner that repenteth, than over ninety and nine just persons who need no repentance. And will he not lend a listening ear to those repentant souls in outer darkness, who are weeping in remorse, or gnashing their teeth in despair? Will he not hear their cry? What is the use of the outer darkness, the awakening to a knowledge of their sin, if it be not for the purpose of repentance on one side, and pardon on the other?

When we can get away from our old and crude ideas of heaven as a place of existence beyond this world only, and realize that it is a *state* of existence, a state of happiness commenced here on this earth; when we realize that eternal life is also commenced here, and that every man who really accepts Christ, and does the will of God, has already entered heaven, and received the gift of eternal life,—we may also be able to understand that eternal death, annihilation, also commences in this world; that the chaos of hell, as well as the kingdom of heaven, is within us; that that also is not a place, but a state of existence, the full misery of which, in the one case, we do not realize here, any more than we experience the full blessings and happiness of heaven, or realize the gift of eternal life, in the other.

Then, what is the resurrection of judgment, and the outer darkness which Christ pictures as the condition of the wicked and unrepentant? Is it not the awakening to a knowledge of our sinfulness, into a realization of our position? Is it not, that the disinthralled spirit now takes cognizance of the sins done in the body? Does it not see the many opportunities lost? Then it is that out of the blackness and darkness of their sinful state, some repent in tears and wailings their past life, their wasted opportunities, and cry for mercy; while others, overwhelmed with a knowledge of their sins, and feeling the impossibility of forgiveness, gnash their teeth with fierce anger and despair. Sin may have had such hold on some, as to have weakened their spiritual being to such an extent that there is no recuperation, and a knowledge of their sinfulness leads to despondency and despair, and their existence ceases; they die the second death.

Let us remember, the *dead* that *hear* shall live.

If the kingdom of heaven begins on this earth,

how are we to know that we have entered therein, and obtained eternal life?

God is love: so, too, is heaven. Love is its life, its being, its atmosphere, its language. Love to God is shown by love to man. "If a man say, I love God, and hateth his brother, he is a liar; for he that loveth not his brother whom he hath seen, cannot love God whom he hath not seen; and this commandment have we from him, that he who loveth God love his brother also." What have you *done to help* your fellow-man, — physically, intellectually, morally, or spiritually? What have you done to increase the happiness of one the least of these my brethren? is the question propounded by Christ; and as your answer is, so is your sentence. And these questions you can answer here and now. Have you given meat to the hungry, and drink to the thirsty? Have you sheltered the stranger, clothed the naked, visited the sick and the prisoner? Have you taught the ignorant, shown God's love to the vile, and instructed the wicked in the ways of truth and holiness? and have you done this, not to save your own life (for he that saveth his life shall lose it), but because of your love for your fellow-men, and from a genuine desire to aid them and do them good? The judgment is passed at once upon you. "My words shall judge you," says Christ. You are your own judge; and as your answer to these questions in the light of the Christ's teachings is yes or no, shall you know whether or not you are in the kingdom of heaven, whether or not you have already received the gift of eternal life. Christ has given this test, and each of us can answer.

Let us remember we cannot do righteousness by proxy after our death: to do righteousness is to live a righteous and holy life. Many a millionnaire holds on to his Lord's money until his last breath, and then endeavors to make a virtue of necessity, and thinks he is doing God a service which will be credited to him, by devising the property, which is not his, for charitable objects. He is thus giving God's money into other hands, that their faithfulness may enure to his benefit. Only while it is in his possession, is it his as trustee for his Lord: when his body dies, his trust ceases. Only while he lives, can he use or abuse the talents God has put into his hands, and for that use or abuse he must answer.

"Know ye not that the unrighteous shall not inherit the kingdom of God?" (1 Cor. vi. 9.)

VI.

OTHER CHRISTIAN SUBJECTS.

ANGELS AND DEVILS, HEAVEN AND HELL.

IN the religion of the Aryas, there was not so much as an intimation or suggestion of a being or power antagonistic to the Deity. No god of evil, Satan, or devil, was known. Nor was there any thing suggestive of hell or of eternal punishment. On the contrary, the image of the cherubim, and the flaming sword turning every way to keep the tree of life, suggests instant destruction, not eternal suffering. Neither did the Christ or his apostles teach the existence of either.

As the Deity, in his initial contract with Abram, met *him* on the par of *his* understanding and belief; and also in the greater contract made with the Hebrews, again, met *them* on the plane of *their* belief, and used it for his own purposes, — so the Christ met the Jews of his time on the plane of *their* belief, and used that belief in illustration of his teachings. Evil was in the world. How it came, was an unsolved problem; the only apparent solution was to charge it to a god of evil, and Satan was the result.

Owing to their belief in Hades, or hell, and in devils and demons, the revelation of the Christ was not so full and free on this point as the original made to the Aryas. It would have been useless for him to have denied the existence of either. In those respects he was confined, but he used these beliefs to emphasize the torments of remorse.

"Hell" is used in the New Testament, both in the sense of the grave, and as the name of an underground abode of spirits (called "sheol" in the new translation). Existence in this place was rather misty and undefined, as well as the object of it.

During their two hundred years of Persian nationality, the religion of the Jews became tinged with the Persian doctrines of the conflicting powers of good and evil.

The self-existent and spiritual God, called by the Persians Ahura-Mazda, was the good power; and Akem-mano, or Satan, was the evil or bad power. These powers had systems of angels, archangels, and powers of light, on the one side, and devils, demons, and powers of darkness, on the other; and these dual gods were supposed to be in constant conflict, through the forces at their command.

In the Jewish writings of that time, we have the first indications of belief in evil personalities or devils; and about the same time are found the first indications of a belief in immortality, and of future reward and punishment.

The Jews do not appear to have applied the idea of a spiritual god to Jehovah. This spiritual god was the god of the Persians, and they did not associate the two: to them they were distinct and separate gods.

This belief in angels and other angelic beings, and in devils and other evil powers, appears three hundred and fifty years later, at the time of Christ, in a modified form.

While the Jews believed in Satan as a power of evil, they did not believe in him as a god, but more as he is represented in the Book of Job (where he is called a son of God), as a being permitted by God to wander to and fro in the earth, to test the faith of mankind by tormenting them with pain, and afflicting them with sickness. Insane persons were believed to be possessed or controlled by devils.

It will be observed that Christ met these diseased persons on the plane of their own and the general belief. He addresses them, and commands the evil spirits to depart from them, with the authority of a master confident of his power. There is no hesitation in the command, nor delay in the result. He shows that, whether it be a sickness, or an actual possession, it is wholly under control; and he gives no aid or comfort to a belief in Satan or devils, as beings beyond the power of God, or of himself as God's messenger and agent.

The idea of Satan and devils, coupled with a place of punishment called hell, are entirely ignored in the teachings of Christ and in the preaching of the apostles and early Christians; but were at a later period introduced as a doctrine of the Christian Church, and in the Dark Ages took shape, intensity, and prominence, in correspondence with the savage and barbarous feelings of the time, when men were guided more by passion and superstition than by reason; when force was the power which ruled the home and the world, and religious zeal enforced a religion of vengeance and hate, miscalled Christian, by war and carnage, by breaking at the wheel, and burning at the stake, and by the wholesale destruction and slaughter of those differing from them on unimportant points of doctrine. This doctrine of the dual gods of good and evil has come down to us. Men even now cling to this belief. Many of them fear the Devil more than they love God; and to use the name of the Devil irreverently meets the same, perhaps heavier reproof than would the like use of the name of the Deity. They scout Christ's teaching of the love of God as impossible and unworthy of him; and many teachers of false Christianity believe the fear of the Devil and hell is more efficacious in bringing souls to repentance than is the long-suffering kindness and tender mercy of our God.

The orthodox hell and Devil is a manufacture of the Dark Ages, intensified by Calvin; a belief entirely different from that of any other people in any age of the world, and wholly unknown to the Jews in the time of Christ, or to the apostles.

Knowing that selfishness, sin, and crime create hell, and that the stings of remorse are much more painful and lasting than the torments of devils, Christ used the belief of his time to color and point his imagery of the punishments of the sinful man thereafter.

Neither Christ nor his apostles taught of a personal Devil. If there is such a personality, he must either be self-existent, — and, if so, then another and antagonistic god, apparently more powerful than God our Father, — or he is a created being. If created, then he is a son of God, created and sustained by him. Without God he cannot live a moment. He cannot antagonize God, except as a wicked man may be said to oppose him. He is wholly and entirely a child of God, and can do nothing but by his permission.

So, too, if God created and sustains this universe and all that is therein, then, if there is such a *place* as hell, it must be in the universe, and wholly under God's control. The devils cannot *exist*, nor hell *be*, without God. He holds them and it in his hands and in his keeping.

Christ was aware that the sufferings of the wicked were much greater than any punishment believed in by the Jews, and that the place where those wicked spirits did congregate was blacker and darker than any "Hades" which the imagination of man had conceived.

He saw human devils, the spirits of the departed wicked, still bound to earth, and employed in tempting men, and urging those on earth in the flesh, who were wickedly inclined, to their spiritual destruction.

He saw the spirits of the selfish, of the rich who had cruelly neglected their duties on earth; had acted as if the riches in their possession belonged to them; and had forgotten that they were only the chosen almoners of God, who had commanded them to aid the distressed, succor the feeble, give to them that are in want, clothe the naked, heal the sick, feed the hungry, in fact, hold the riches in their hands as the servants of the most high God, the bestowers of his bounty. He saw these bound to the earth by their interest in this god of their worship; one watching the spendthrift son, while squandering *his* money, sink deeper and deeper into the depths of sin and iniquity, — the result of his own sinful neglect of his duties as a father. Another watching the sorrows of many whom he had known on the earth, while they struggled against sickness and discouragements; those to whom a gift of a few hundreds or thousands of his former hoarded wealth would have been a blessing which would have encouraged them, and placed them above want; and thousands of others who might have been helped by him, and whose benedictions would have gladdened his soul.

He saw the hypocrite, who on earth had been loud in professions, and given to long prayers, but who had secretly cheated the rich and robbed the poor, now unable to even raise his eyes in prayer; with his soul in all its blackness in full view before him, his secret sins exposed not only to himself but to all others, with his deadened conscience alive and stinging him.

He saw the favored of fortune, the high-liver, the good fellow, so-called, with his whole selfish, wicked, licentious life before him, bowed down in humiliation and shame; overwhelmed with remorse; unable in his despair to utter even the publican's prayer, "God be merciful to me a sinner."

Such as these, and worse, were the scenes open to the eyes of the Christ; and is it any wonder that he should use the strongest types of suffering to portray to man the terrible punishment of the impenitent wicked?

These were the devils, and these the hells, opened to the spiritual sight of the Christ.

But there were other sights. If hell is within man, so also is heaven. Of children he says, "Their angels do always behold the face of my Father which is in heaven." They were under the tender care of the spirits of the blest.

If the spirits of the wicked are able to influence the souls of those on earth, who, by dwelling on evil, and harboring impure and wicked thoughts, desires, and purposes, invite their entrance; in the same manner, the spirits of the lovely and pure can influence those who inwardly desire and seek for good.

The spirits of the loved and lost on earth still hover around us, ready with their aid and help, with their suggestions of good; and the power of these spirits is great for the benefit of those whom they love and care for. There is no hell so deep, no sinner so foul, no suffering so great, that these angelic workers of God cannot penetrate the depth so deep, reach the sinner so foul, and endeavor to turn the sufferer to his Father who ever loveth him, and hath compassion on his suffering, and is ready to pardon his sins.

God is not willing that any should perish, but that all should receive eternal life.

"All souls are mine," saith the Lord; and "none shall take them out of my Father's hands," saith the Christ.

Death merely relieves the human being of its covering of flesh. The man is the same the day after that he was the day before his disrobement; but in the removal of his fleshly covering, man is exposed naked to his own gaze, and to the sight of the spirits around him.

See the abasement of the self-righteous man, the horror of the murderer, the deep degradation of the licentious, the suffering of the selfish, the despair of those who have wasted their gifts and opportunities. See them as they follow the effect of their sins on others in the ever-widening wave of eternity, and imagine, if you can, their terror and shame; imagine how they are weighed down by remorse; imagine what a tremendous effort is necessary for them, in view of their sins, to raise a thought or prayer to Him whose laws they have so outraged and disobeyed.

See, too, the meek, the humble, the lowly, as he

awakes to a knowledge of himself, and raises a prayer of thankfulness to Him who has preserved him. See him who has used his talents, whether one or ten, for the benefit of others; who has given of his riches, whether much or little, to those in need; him whose sympathy has been shown in kind deeds and expressions of love. See those who have worked for the benefit of mankind, whose love of God was shown by love of man. See these as they hear the benediction of the Master: "Inasmuch as ye have done it unto one the least of these my brethren, ye have done it unto me; enter thou into the joy of your Lord." See them as they rise with countenances illumined with happiness, enter into the realm of joy and peace, and say, is the contrast too great between the hell and the heaven which man makes for himself?

Hell is selfishness, heaven is love.

Every man makes his own hell or his own heaven. He is the judge, and he goes to either as he decides on earth.

Were it not for the mercy of God, and the love of man, there would be no release from the woes of hell. But the spirits in bliss cannot be supremely happy while those whom they love are suffering in hell.

These spirits of the just, these angels of heaven,

are all earnest workers for the happiness of others, and they strive not only with man on earth, but with those in hell; working with all the earnestness of their being, to bring the sinful soul to repentance; encouraging him in doubt, aiding him in despair, praying for him in his agony and remorse, working on with love and hope, never giving up until the suffering soul has raised its prayer to God for help, and through trouble, pain, and travail of spirit has been forgiven and received into that blest abode, where there is more joy over one sinner that repenteth, than over ninety and nine just (innocent) persons that need no repentance.

MIRACLES.

Webster defines a miracle as "an effect or event contrary to the established constitution and course of things, — a deviation from the known laws of nature."

"Natural laws," he says, "are the agencies which carry on the processes of creation." Any thing supernatural is "beyond or exceeding the powers of nature."

A deviation changes nothing. It is not a new law, or the overturning of an old law. It is merely a change of direction for a special purpose, a swerving from the regular and generally observed course.

A miracle, then, may not be a supernatural act or event; it may only be a deviation from the usual exhibition of the laws of nature, not a change in the law itself; these deviations being an apparent change to *us* only, it being in the power of that God who formed the laws of nature, to govern and control each individual creation of his hands. These laws are wholly under his control, subject to his command. He is their Master, not they his. He can use them for his purposes, and to further his designs; and in the Bible we have the record of such deviations, made, as we believe, for sufficient cause.

Man makes a machine to do certain work. The action of this machine is governed by certain laws applicable to itself as a machine, but these do not affect the maker. He may alter, improve, or add other powers, without violating any law to which he is responsible. The machine may have certain hidden powers, only brought into action by emergencies. It may work on for years in its regular course. Suddenly the emergency arises; and a new action takes place, provided for when it was made, but not used, and perhaps to lookers-on unknown, until this time. Is this new action a miracle? No. It is only a deviation from its usual action, brought out by the exigencies of the occasion.

God makes the laws of nature the "agencies which carry on the processes of creation." It is evident there was a time when these laws, as applied to this earth, were few as compared with the present.

The first plant created was an addition to the previously existing creation, and required a new law to sustain and keep it in being; and this law was an addition to the pre-existing laws of nature. The first fish, bird, animal, man, were each and all new creations, requiring new laws for each to regulate their continuance. Thus were the laws formed. A part of these were the laws of reproduction, each of its kind. When they took effect, and the young plant sprang from the seed, although a part of the law, it was a new appearance. Each beast, bird, man, was formed mature, and the first-born of each was a deviation because none such had previously appeared. Apparently these deviations were miracles, but in reality they were only new exhibitions of laws already established.

Nature is a machine made by God, and governed by his laws. God is not only the Maker, but the Master, of those laws. New, strange, and unexpected powers have been hidden for a time, but acted when the necessities of the new creations required it. Man finds in the water, in the air, in the mineral and vegetable kingdoms, new powers and new forms of life, all miracles in the sense of being new and before-undiscovered products, but really only deviations from the old results. The miracles of the Bible may be but "deviations from the known laws of nature," "events contrary to the established course of things."

In the ignorance and superstition of the times of Moses, God could appeal only to the senses of the Hebrew people or the Egyptian nation. Miracle, so-called, was the only power which would work upon the fears of the Egyptians, cause them to release the Hebrews from bondage, and embolden them to take their liberty.

Is it not presumptuous for man to speak of miracles as impossible? They may be beyond what he has *known* of nature's laws. A hundred years ago, what did man know of the laws of electricity? Are all the various exhibitions of its powers and uses now discovered, miracles? They are additions to, or deviations from, the then known laws.

Are the powers of steam miracles, because only a hundred years ago its only known use was to make the kettle sing? Is the telephone a miracle because it has developed new laws of acoustics?

God's "laws of nature" are expansive, progressive. If we find these laws of nature have enlarged, and are still enlarging, is it not natural to suppose, as a man advances, and other powers now unknown become his, that these laws shall continue to enlarge, and new laws be discovered, so that these deviations may become known as laws, and miracles become common facts, as these other deviations from the laws we have mentioned have become facts?

A miracle was received by the Jew with unquestioned faith. It was the direct action of Jehovah. In former times it had been performed generally in some exigency of their national life; at times in its early history, in punishment for disobedience of his law; but generally for their rescue or protection, and to spread the terror of his name among the nations. Their birth as a nation had been accomplished by the most stupendous miracles. The rule of Moses had been enforced by other miracles. Their support for forty years in the wilderness had been a daily miracle. Their occupation of Canaan had been accompanied by frequent miracles; and in times of trouble, through all their early history, the hand of Jehovah had been opened to help whenever they sincerely trusted in him. To eliminate the miraculous element from the Hebrew and Christian Scriptures, would be to leave the covers only in the hands of the operator.

That the Hebrews claimed miraculous help in many events which to us appear to have been accomplished by natural laws, or as the result of good generalship, does not affect the fact that the largest number of these occurrences could have been accomplished by no other than supernatural power. The whole history of the nation avows it, and no disbelief or scoff of sceptics can shake the accumulative evidence recorded in the entire history of the nation.

Man has been given and has wielded an apparently supernatural power, a power above and controlling the laws of nature.

This power emanating from God, — which is called in the Bible the Holy Spirit, — embodying the purpose, force, energy, power, the enlightening wisdom and love of God, this supernatural power, has at times been given into the hands of man. It was used in its energy and force by Moses and by Elijah; in its enlightening power, by Isaiah and other prophets; and for beneficent purposes, and in the exhibition of the love of God, by Jesus the Christ and his disciples. This spiritual power we believe to be still reserved for the use of man, when in singleness of purpose, and self-devotedness, and in communion with God, he shall ask the aid of the Deity in restoring health and strength to suffering humanity.

The power of mind over matter has been long known and acknowledged. What is that but the power of the spiritual controlling the natural?

The same power is seen in the various well-authenticated cases of the cure of disease by faith, by prayer, by the laying-on of hands, and by the Christian Science apostles. All are but exhibitions of the control of the natural by the spiritual, of the natural laws by the spiritual laws known in the Bible as the Holy Spirit.

THE CRUCIFIXION.

Jesus of Nazareth was chosen from among God's children, consecrated and enlightened by the Holy Spirit to reveal the being and character of God, and his purposes or intentions with respect to the being, position, and future life of man.

Other sons of God had been chosen before the Christ, for certain work. Abraham, with whom the first or personal contract or covenant was made; Moses, to whom the Deity was revealed as Jehovah, and through whom the Hebrew contract was made; the prophets, through whom God revealed his will and purposes with regard to the future of individuals and nations on this earth, — all were chosen sons of God, each selected and enlightened by the Holy Spirit sufficiently to carry out the will and purposes of the Deity.

While the contract made with Abraham was personal to himself, his family and descendants, and that made with the Hebrews was national, confined wholly to that nation, and earthly in its character, the revelation and contract made through Jesus of Nazareth as the Christ, the Messiah, the Son of God, chosen for and consecrated to that purpose, was wholly spiritual, filling out the former revelations, and surpassing them in all things, as heaven surpasses earth. This contract or covenant is open to all mankind. Jew and Gentile, high and low, rich and poor, all are called upon to accept the revelations of the Christ, and join in the contract which he offers to all, not of earthly power, riches, or grandeur, but of heavenly riches and eternal life.

It was not until Jesus of Nazareth had received the recognition of God, and the consecration and enlightenment of the Holy Spirit, that he began to teach; and he then taught, not as Jesus of Nazareth, but as the Christ, the Son of God, chosen and anointed for that purpose. He at all times confessed that his knowledge and his power came entirely from God, that of himself he could do nothing. While calling himself the Son of God, he took particular pains to acknowledge himself the Son of man, that all mankind were his brothers and with him sons of God; and spoke of God as "*our* Father," and in addressing others called him "*your* Father." In no way did Jesus the Christ differ from other men, except in being selected and chosen from among men to fill the office of the Christ.

It was as the Christ, and only as the Christ, that he taught. It was the enlightening power of the Holy Spirit which gave him the certainty of knowledge, and caused him to teach with authority. It is that only which causes us to have faith in his teachings, which gives a foundation for our belief. Take away this certainty, this authority, and of what value are his teachings? They are merely the guesses, the vain imaginings, of a poor illiterate peasant of Galilee, a place noted for its poverty and the ignorance of its people; and they have no force or power to enlighten or aid man. Take away this authority, and we are without God as well as without Christ in the world.

All spiritual knowledge comes directly from the Christ: it can be obtained from no other source. Men believe in the voice of nature, in the love and fatherhood of God, in the brotherhood of man, in the kingdom of heaven, and in the future life, because of the certainty of his teachings; and that certainty comes only from the actual knowledge received from God by the Christ, the chosen and anointed Son of God.

Christ's work was initiatory: he enunciated the doctrines we have mentioned, and left them for his disciples to spread abroad throughout the world, when they should become aware of their power and value.

Christ's teachings were new; they were strange. The people did not comprehend them. Even his disciples failed to understand their meaning. Notwithstanding his constant teachings, the kingdom of heaven they still thought was to be an earthly reign of Christ. Even to the last they disputed upon the positions they were to hold in this new kingdom; and after his resurrection, they ask him, "Lord, wilt thou at this time restore again the kingdom to Israel?" They disbelieved when he spoke of his death. Christ was to live and reign forever: he could not die. When they actually saw him expire on the cross, their faith failed: they fled to their homes dismayed and disheartened. He could not have been the Christ, or he would not have died.

The continuance of life after the decease of the body was believed in by the Pharisees. The Sadducees disbelieved it; the common people generally gave it but little thought. Those who believed in the doctrine, did so with fear and trembling. There was no certainty; it was the mere guess-work of those who desired and longed for it, or the faith was a relic borrowed from Persia.

Moses knew nothing of a life hereafter, and never taught it. All his laws are connected with this life, and the rewards and punishments are wholly human and earthly.

This question, however, troubled other minds besides the Jews. Many among the heathen nations were making the inquiry, "If a man die, shall he live again?"

There was a belief among the heathen of a shadowy state of existence after death, but no certainty; and who could answer the question? Neither the gods of Greece or Rome, nor did the Jehovah of the Jews answer it. Men were groping blindly for a solution of the question. Many of the thoughtful minds of all nations were seeking light. Some had boldly declared their belief in a future state, and others as boldly denied the possibility of it.

If there was such a life beyond, did it belong to all mankind as their birthright? or was it, as some believed, reserved for the few who, by reason of great and benevolent work for man, received the blessing of the gods and the gift of immortality? Could it be secured by assenting to certain forms of belief, or by following certain religious observances? Could it be obtained by mortifying the flesh, and living a life of self-denial? No one knew; and no one could answer with any certainty the question, "What shall I do to obtain eternal life?"

Christ came: he revealed the certainty of life eternal, and showed how each and all might obtain it. He claimed to teach from personal knowledge, that he uttered the words of God; that he was the messenger of God. His teachings bore the impress of sincerity and the stamp of authority. Yet how could he know? Were men to believe because of his assertions? Could he have been taught of God? Was such a thing possible? His miracles gave evidence of a power beyond that of man. Did that power come from God? or was he a deceiver, and did he obtain his power from the Evil One, as was charged by the Pharisees?

Christ's revelation, his teaching, needed confirmation, and this could only be obtained by ocular demonstration. The dead must arise again from the grave.

This had been done in a partial manner. The daughter of Jairus had been raised from the dead; the son of the woman of Nain had been brought to life after he had been prepared for burial; and, more wonderful than all, Lazarus, after lying four days in the tomb, had been raised, and returned to his sorrowing sisters in life and health. But here might be collusion. What proof was there of his death? Had not Jesus himself said, "He is not dead, but sleepeth"?

Christ from the first saw the necessity of this sacrifice, — saw that he must die in order that he might show the resurrection from the dead. He foretold it, but his disciples did not believe him. Yet he constantly pressed towards it: it was to be the crowning act of his life, the seal of his ministry, the great proof of his sincerity and truth, the confirmation of all his teaching. He claimed to have the power to lay down his life, and to take it again. He was free to act: would he do it? As the time approached, he naturally shrank from the infamy, disgrace, and pain of the cross; he prayed that the cup might pass from him, that some other way might be opened to accomplish the same result. But in vain: if he would accomplish the work given him to do, he must die for men, that, through his death and resurrection, they might learn that the soul is immortal, that the death of the body has no effect on the spiritual being inhabiting that body.

It was necessary that his death should be public: all the Jewish world should be cognizant of it. The Roman rulers must be aware of it; it must be so public and notorious that there could be no dispute respecting it.

Christ's miracles had made him the centre of observation. Wherever he came, the sick and infirm were brought unto him, and he healed them. He entered Jerusalem accompanied by thousands. He was greeted as a king; palm-branches were spread before him, and shouts of welcome filled the air. But in a few days he was seized, and, after a mock trial, was condemned, and executed on the cross.

This execution was public; and owing to the preceding publicity of his life, acts, and teaching, the circumstances of his entry into Jerusalem, and the excitement at his trial, it was known to all Jerusalem, and to the thousands that were present from all parts of the world attending the great festival.

. . . .

Apparently Christ's work on earth was ended. He who claimed to be the Son of God had been put to death, and that was the end. His disciples were dispersed, and all their hopes destroyed.

Had this been the end indeed, what would have become of the teachings of Christ? What would have been his influence on the earth? We probably should never have heard of him, or of his teachings. His few ignorant disciples, frightened and disheartened, would have gone each to his own home, and resumed his former occupation. Christ's teachings would have been forgotten, and himself would have passed into oblivion. His principal work had been done in an obscure portion of Palestine, a Roman province or dependency, among a people uncultivated and despised by both Grecian and Roman. The rumors which might have reached the more civilized portion of the world, of wonderful works performed by a man whom some called a prophet and others a deceiver, would have died away. He left no writings; he had formed no school of philosophy; his teaching had been oral, misunderstood or disbelieved; and his death ended both his teaching and his influence. Possibly some tales of his miracles and tragic death might have come down to us, in some myth or fabulous story; but his life and teaching would have been lost to the world.

But we, — mankind in general, — what would we be? Ignorant savages, or possibly worshippers of the thousand gods of Greece and Rome, perhaps farther advanced in civilization, probably sunk in the darkness and crime of the Canaanites, with no knowledge of God, no immortal life, and no desire for either.

In these days, liberal writers place great stress upon the voice of nature; that nature leads man to a knowledge of God. But who taught us that there was a God who was the Lord of nature?

that he was the maker and sustainer of the universe? Who but the Christ?

Previous to the Christ, there were gods without number, but no God, — no Deity supreme. The national god of the Jews, Jehovah, was, in our view, the greatest and most powerful of them all, but not so acknowledged by the world at that time. He was, in fact, unknown, except to this small and almost uncivilized nation; while the gods of Rome ruled the world. Nature was ruled by a host of gods; but the God of the Christ — the fountain of all our religious knowledge — was unknown and unthought of.

How has this death of the Christ, and his resurrection, been covered and hid under the creeds and theologies of man, as were the laws of Moses under the traditions of the elders!

This crowning act of his life, this open way to immortality, has been turned into the sacrifice of a god, who took upon himself the sins of mankind, and expiated their sins by his death upon the cross. If he was God, then his death was impossible, and the whole thing was a farce acted to deceive. If he was a man, then he could not take upon himself the sins of others, and his death did not relieve them from the punishment belonging to sin. Besides, if it could, where was the greatness of the sacrifice? Are there not men now, to-day, thousands of them, who, if they could relieve the world from sin by so doing, would gladly undergo the same suffering and death?

The death and resurrection of Christ was the beginning of the gospel; all else was preliminary. Without this there would have been no Christ: he would never have been heard of. His disciples would never have preached a dead Christ, and his doctrines would have died with him.

The cross, the instrument of his death, became the symbol of life, not of death. The living Christ, Christ arisen, was the rallying cry of the apostles, the burden of their teaching, and their joyful song.

All the writers of the New Testament unite in their testimony to his death; and there is no point so strongly and fully proved as this in the life of Jesus of Nazareth, the Christ of God.

All the apostles testify to the crucifixion and death of Christ.

Matthew says, " And when they had crucified him, they parted his garments among them, casting lots " (xxvii. 35).

" Jesus cried again with a loud voice, and yielded up his spirit" (xxvii. 50).

Mark's testimony is, "And they crucified him, and parted his garments among them, casting lots upon them what each should take. And it was the third hour, and they crucified him " (xv. 24).

"And Jesus uttered a loud voice, and gave up the ghost" (xv. 37).

Luke testifies, "And when they came unto the place which is called the skull, there they crucified him" (xxiii. 33).

"And when Jesus had cried with a loud voice, he said, Father, into thy hands I commend my spirit; and having said this, he gave up the ghost" (xxiii. 46).

And the testimony of John is to the same effect: "They took Jesus, therefore, and he went out bearing the cross for himself, into the place called the place of a skull, which is called in Hebrew Golgotha; where they crucified him" (xix. 17, 18).

"When Jesus, therefore, had received the vinegar, he said, It is finished: and he bowed his head, and gave up his spirit" (xix. 30).

Peter charges the Jews, without their dissent: "Him, being delivered up by the determinate counsel and foreknowledge of God, ye by the hand of lawless men did crucify and slay." (Acts ii. 23.)

"Let all the house of Israel therefore know assuredly, that God hath made him both Lord and Christ, this Jesus whom ye crucified." (Acts ii. 36.)

And Paul frequently speaks of it. "We preach Christ crucified." (1 Cor. i. 23.)

"For I determined not to know any thing among you, save Jesus Christ and him crucified." (1 Cor. ii. 2.)

"Which none of the rulers of this world knoweth; for, had they known it, they would not have crucified the Lord of glory." (1 Cor. ii. 8.)

"For he was crucified through weakness, yet he liveth through the power of God." (2 Cor. xiii. 4.)

"O foolish Galatians, who did bewitch you, before whose eyes Jesus Christ was openly set forth crucified?" (Gal. iii. 1.)

"For Christ sent me, not to baptize, but to preach the gospel: not in wisdom of words, lest the cross of Christ should be made void. For the word of the cross is to them that are perishing foolishness: but unto us which are being saved it is the power of God. For it is written, —

"I will destroy the wisdom of the wise,

"And the prudence of the prudent will I reject.

"Where is the wise? Where is the scribe? Where is the disputer of this world? Hath not God made foolish the wisdom of the world? For seeing that in the wisdom of God the world through its wisdom knew not God, it was God's good pleasure through the foolishness of the preaching, to save them that believe. Seeing that Jews ask for signs, and Greeks seek after wisdom: but we preach Christ crucified, unto Jews a stumbling-block, and unto Gentiles foolishness; but unto them that are called, both Jews and Greeks, Christ the power of God, and the wisdom of God." (1 Cor. i. 17-25.)

THE RESURRECTION.

But the great and grand event in the life of Christ is his resurrection; and this again was almost as public as his execution had been.

His crucifixion had not taken place in a corner, but in the full public gaze. At his death there were rumors abroad, that he had said he would arise again from the tomb. So prominent had they become, that the chief priests and Pharisees, believing there would be an attempt by his disciples to obtain his body, applied to the governor for a guard to watch the tomb in which he had been laid. At their request, a small body of Roman soldiers were placed on guard, after the entrance to the tomb had been sealed. They testified to the appearance of the angel, and the opening of the tomb. The women and Peter and John saw the empty grave; and all the apostles, together with many believers beside, testified to his re-appearance, and to his teaching among them for a period of forty days, and of his final ascension.

The excitement, indignation, and sorrow caused by his crucifixion had not subsided, before these tales of his return to life were spread abroad; and soon the men who had been his disciples appeared, and fearlessly proclaimed the doctrine of the resurrection from the dead, and eternal life, based upon this resurrection of Christ from the dead, of which they were witnesses. These statements they made publicly in Jerusalem, in the very city where he had been put to death; and they charged the Jewish people with being criminally cognizant of, and consenting to, his death. And this charge was not denied. On the contrary, it was acknowledged; and the conviction of its truth was so strong, that the multitude cried out to the apostles, "Men and brethren, what shall we do?"

The testimony to the resurrection of Christ is very full and direct, and cannot be doubted, except we believe every writer to be a falsifier.

Christ repeatedly foretold his resurrection. This was so well known, that after his crucifixion "the chief priests and the Pharisees were gathered together unto Pilate saying, Sir, we remember that that deceiver said, while he was yet alive, After three days I rise again. Command therefore that the sepulchre be made sure until the third day, lest haply his disciples come and steal him away, and say unto the people, He is risen from the dead; and the last error will be worse than the first. Pilate said unto them, Ye have a guard: go your way, make it as sure as ye can. So they went, and made the sepulchre sure, sealing the stone, the guard being with them."

"Now late on the sabbath day, as it began to dawn towards the first day of the week, came Mary Magdalene, and the other Mary, to see the sepulchre. And, behold, there was a great earthquake; for an angel of the Lord descended from heaven, and came and rolled away the stone, and sat upon it. His appearance was as lightning, and his raiment white as snow: and for fear of him the watchers did quake, and became as dead men.

"And the angel answered and said unto the women, Fear not ye: for I know that ye seek Jesus, which hath been crucified. He is not here; for he is risen, even as he said. Come, see the place where the Lord lay. And go quickly, and tell his disciples, He is risen from the dead; and lo, he goeth before you into Galilee; there shall ye see him: lo, I have told you. And they departed quickly from the tomb with fear and great joy, and ran to bring his disciples word. And behold, Jesus met them, saying, All hail. And they came and took hold of his feet, and worshipped him. Then saith Jesus unto them, Fear not: go tell my brethren that they depart into Galilee, and there shall they see me.

"Now, while they were going, behold, some of the guard came into the city, and told unto the chief priests all the things that were come to pass. And when they were assembled with the elders, and had taken counsel, they gave large money unto the soldiers, saying, Say ye, His disciples came by night, and stole him away while we slept. And if this come to the governor's ears, we will persuade him, and rid you of care. So they took the money, and did as they were taught; and this saying was spread abroad among the Jews, and continueth until this day." (Matt. xxviii. 1–15.)

This account of the resurrection, given by Matthew, is sustained by Mark, Luke, and John, who agree substantially with the statement here given; varying somewhat, as would naturally be the case, in the minor details, and adding other incidents which came to their knowledge. They also agree in stating that Christ met with the disciples after his resurrection, and that he taught them that they might understand the Scriptures. He showed them from the Scriptures, "that the Christ should suffer, and rise again from the dead the third day; and that repentance and remission of sins should be preached in his name unto all the nations."

The apostles testify to the resurrection of Jesus the Christ from the dead, and make it the foundation of their teaching, the proof of the truth of their gospel of good tidings.

The eleven disciples, after the ascension of Christ, met to choose a disciple in the place ot Judas Iscariot. "Of the men therefore which have companied with us all the time that the Lord Jesus went in and went out among us, beginning from the baptism of John, unto the day that he was *received up from us*, of these must one become a witness with us of his resurrection." (Acts i. 22, 23.) Not of his life, or his death, but of his resurrection.

Peter says, speaking of Jesus the Christ, —

" Whom God raised up, having loosed the pangs of death : because it was not possible that he should be holden of it." (Acts ii. 24.)

" The priests and the captain of the temple and the Sadducees came upon them, being sore troubled because they taught the people, and proclaimed in Jesus the resurrection from the dead." (Acts iv. 2.)

" And with great power gave the apostles their witness of the resurrection of the Lord Jesus." (Acts iv. 33.)

" Blessed be the God and Father of our Lord Jesus Christ, who according to his abundant mercy hath begotten us again unto a lively hope by the resurrection of Jesus Christ from the dead." (1 Pet. i. 3.)

Paul gives frequent and powerful testimony to the resurrection of Jesus the Christ from the dead.

"And certain also of the Epicurean and Stoic philosophers encountered him. And some said, What would this babbler say? Other some, He seemeth to be a setter forth of strange gods: because he preached Jesus and the resurrection." (Acts xvii. 18.)

"Now, when they heard of the resurrection of the dead, some mocked; but others said, We will hear thee concerning this yet again." (Acts xvii. 32.)

"Who was declared to be the Son of God with power, according to the spirit of holiness, by the resurrection of the dead; even Jesus Christ our Lord." (Rom. i. 4.)

"For if we have become united with him by the likeness of his death, we shall be also by the likeness of his resurrection." (Rom. vi. 5.)

The foundation of all the preaching of the apostles is well given in Paul's argument to the Corinthians, upon the resurrection of the dead: —

"Now, if Christ is preached that he hath been raised from the dead, how say some among you that there is no resurrection of the dead? But if there is no resurrection of the dead, neither hath Christ been raised; and if Christ hath not been raised, then is our preaching vain, your faith also is vain. Yea, and we are found false witnesses of God: because we witnessed of God that he raised up Christ; whom he raised not up, if so be that the dead are not raised. For if the dead are not raised, neither hath Christ been raised; and if Christ hath not been raised, your faith is vain; ye are yet in your sins." (1 Cor. xv. 12-17.)

In his address to the Athenians, Paul says, "The times of ignorance therefore God overlooked; but now he commandeth men that they should all everywhere repent, inasmuch as he hath appointed a day in the which he will judge the world in righteousness by the man whom he hath ordained; whereof he hath given assurance unto all men, in that he hath raised him from the dead." (Acts xvii. 31.)

"But this I confess unto thee, that after the way which they call a sect, so serve I the God of our fathers, believing all things which are according to the law, and which are written in the prophets: having hope toward God, which these also themselves look for, that there shall be a resurrection both of the just and unjust." (Acts xxiv. 14, 15.)

When before Felix, Paul declares his innocence of all wrong-doing, "except it be for this one voice, . . . Touching the resurrection of the dead I am called in question before you this day." Festus reports the matter to King Agrippa: "When the accusers stood up, they brought no charge of such evil things as I supposed; but had certain questions against him of their own religion, and of one Jesus, who was dead, whom Paul affirmed to be alive." And before King Agrippa he says, "Wherefore, O King Agrippa, I was not disobedient unto the heavenly vision: but declared both to them of Damascus first, and at Jerusalem, and throughout all the country of Judæa, and also to the Gentiles, that they should repent and turn to God, doing works worthy of repentance. . . . Having, therefore, obtained the help that is from God, I stand unto this day testifying both to small and great, saying nothing but what the prophets and Moses did say should come, how that the Christ must suffer, and how that he first by the resurrection of the dead should proclaim light both to the people and to the Gentiles." (Acts xxvi. 19-23.)

"Paul, a servant of Jesus Christ, called to be an apostle, separated unto the gospel of God, which he promised afore by his prophets in the holy scriptures, concerning his Son, who was born of the seed of David according to the flesh, who was declared to be the Son of God with power according to the spirit of holiness, by the resurrection of the dead, even Jesus Christ our Lord." (Rom. i. 1–4.)

"Wherefore let us cease to speak of the first principles of Christ, and press on unto perfection, not laying again a foundation of repentance from dead works, and faith toward God, even the teaching of baptisms, and of laying on of hands, and of resurrection of the dead, and of eternal judgment; and this will we do if God permit." (Heb. vi. 1–3.)

THE DISCIPLES.

We have endeavored to make plain the beliefs and expectations of the Jews respecting their Christ; that, as the son of their god Jehovah, he should rule over Israel, and through them over the whole earth, in the same manner that Rome at that time governed the civilized world; and this rule or government they called the rule, government, or kingdom of heaven.

They believed that this Christ would wield the whole power of Jehovah his father; and as, in former contests of Jehovah with the gods of Egypt, their national god had conquered, so now they had full confidence in his ability to overpower the gods of Rome, and thus obtain supreme rule.

As a nation, their hopes, fears, expectations, were all confined to this earth. With the exception of the small sect of Pharisees, they had no knowledge of or belief in a future state of being.

They had never shown any spirituality. While there had been prophets and teachers of a high moral tone, they as a nation had never responded to their teachings. Before their captivity they had worshipped the gods of the nations around them, to the neglect of Jehovah; since their captivity, taught by the lessons of the past as exhibited to them by Ezra, Nehemiah, and others, they had not departed from the outward worship of Jehovah, but theirs were blind offerings, made according to their rituals, with the expectation that the blood of lambs and other animals would wash away sin.

This was the people from among whom Jesus selected his disciples; they were from the common people, of about the same grade of life as was Jesus himself. They had the ideas, wishes, expectations, and prejudices of their nation. Perhaps Jesus could not, if he had tried, have obtained disciples from the higher or more learned classes. He did not come with the regal power, pomp, and magnificence which *they* expected from the Christ. They looked upon him with scorn and contempt, and upon his followers as a few poor, deluded, ignorant peasants and fishermen; just the sort of men who would be likely to be attracted by an impostor.

And these disciples, — were they more enlightened than their countrymen? Did they look upon the Christ in a light differing from the rest of their Jewish race?

As we carefully read the Gospels, we must acknowledge that we find no evidence of a clearer estimate of the Christ or of his work.

Christ spoke of God as our Father, the Father of the whole human race. His disciples believed that Jehovah was the father of the Christ; but when he spoke of him as "our Father," and "your Father," they did not understand him. *They* were not the children of Jehovah; they had never thought of such a thing, and they could not believe it; it was, in fact, blasphemy to entertain such a thought.

Neither did they believe that the heathen nations were children of Jehovah: in fact, they believed that all of them were his enemies, worshippers of other gods, whom he would willingly destroy; he hated Romans more especially; would that the time had come to sweep them from the face of the earth, or at any rate make them tributary to Israel.

The sayings of the Christ were incomprehensible. He taught that the kingdom of heaven was at hand. Yes, they believed that. Was not he the Christ, the Anointed, he who was to establish this kingdom? Were they not awaiting with impatience his movements? Why did he not proclaim himself king, put on his royal robes, gather the nation together, seize and destroy the Romans, and, by the aid of Jehovah, overpower all opposition, and govern the world?

The Christ revealed an immortal life. This they believed. The Christ was immortal. He partook of the nature of his Father Jehovah. He would live forever, and his reign would be without end. This immortality, however, was to be on this earth. As, in later days, Ponce de Leon sought the waters of youth that he might bathe therein and obtain immortal youth, so the disciples believed that the Christ had received from his Father that water and that bread which would give to those who partook thereof immortal life. He was to live forever on this earth, and they desired to live with him; and they awaited with eagerness the time when he should show unto them the way of eternal life, and give to them of that well-spring of immortality.

We do not find that the disciples were spiritually enlightened by the teachings of the Christ. The Sermon on the Mount fell on dull ears; even the simplest of his parables required explanation.

Pre-occupied as were their minds by the prophecies, traditions, and expectations of their nation, which had been instilled into their minds all their lives, they could not and did not understand his teachings. Why should they? They were Jews, not above the average of their race. All that they heard was colored by the medium of their habit of thought; and every saying of Jesus was qualified by their belief in his earthly kingdom and reign.

Only a few days previous to his crucifixion, they disputed with each other as to the position or rank they should hold in his kingdom, the establishment of which, they now felt, must be near at hand.

Apparently, nothing but the death of the Christ could awaken them from this dream of royalty. In their belief, the Christ could not die. If Jesus of Nazareth should die, that would be proof to them, and to the whole Jewish world, that he was not the Christ. No matter what his power over sickness and death had been; if he died, his cause was crushed, annihilated. He could not be the real Christ, but an impostor.

To the surprise and consternation of the disciples, the Christ died on the cross. His death was made doubly sure by the thrust of the spear in his heart.

In dismay, his disciples fled; the laughing-stock, as they thought, of the whole nation. The man whom they had followed, and believed in as the Christ, was proved to be an impostor. Their position as chosen followers of Jesus made them now unpleasantly conspicuous; in silence and despair they slunk away, to hide their sorrow and shame from all mankind.

Thus ended, as they thought, the life of one whom they had loved and revered because of his loving and humane disposition, his kindness, gentleness, and forgiving spirit. Added to their sorrow for his loss, was their disappointment. Jesus, it was proved, was not the Christ, and they and their nation must look for another. The glorious reign of their great king was still in the future, and their hopes were blasted and gone. Nothing remained but to hide their friend in the tomb, and then return to their old trades and occupations.

At this time, had these disciples any thing to teach? Nothing. Not a single truth uttered by the Christ had been spiritually discerned. His personal traits, and the expectation of future greatness, had kept them together, and had been their bond of union: but his death severed the tie; he and his teachings were dead together.

The preachings of both John and Jesus were

illusive; they had either fraudulently or mistakenly proclaimed an untruth. The kingdom of heaven had not come, neither was it at hand. Eternal life was a myth; its apostle had been slain; the water and the bread of life had been powerless. Their friend and teacher, and, as they had believed, their Messiah, had perished on the cross; and the visions of glory, of power, of eternal life, had faded and gone; and this was the end.

Who among his followers would now attempt to preach a dead Christ, and he a malefactor? What had they to teach? Jesus of Nazareth could not be the Messiah: the Christ could not die; yet this man was dead. Of what consequence were his teachings, his revelations? They were the mere vagaries of a disordered mind, of a religious enthusiast. He was dead, and his teachings and so-called revelations would die with him. No man would trouble himself to repeat or publish them to the world; they would sink into oblivion; and the disgrace of his death would attach to his life, and be visited on his disciples.

THE APOSTLES.

Apparently, the teachings of Jesus had come to an end with his life. The Jews had proved that he was an impostor, by depriving him of life.

The Christ had foretold his resurrection. His

disciples had given no heed to this statement, because they did not believe in his death. His enemies, however, remembered his saying; and, thinking his disciples might attempt to take away the body at night, they caused a watch of Roman soldiery to be set about the tomb in which his body had been placed.

In the early morning, these soldiers appeared in the city, thoroughly frightened, and told a confused story of an earthquake that had removed the stone from the mouth of the tomb, and of angels whose presence had caused them to flee in terror.

Some of the women, who had gone to prepare the body for burial, sought Peter and John with the news that the body of Jesus had disappeared; that in the tomb they had seen angels, who informed them that the Christ had arisen, and that he would meet them in Galilee.

This news again brought the disciples together, filled with wonder and hope. Would he now take possession of his kingdom? Would he now restore Israel? These were the questions which came to their lips.

We have no record of the teachings of the forty days, during which he explained to his disciples the spiritual bearing of his teachings. He spoke to them of the Father; of the spiritual kingdom of heaven, or the rule of God in the heart; of the eternal life of the spirit, freed from the prison of the mortal body; and of the way to obtain immortality.

The resurrection of the Christ was the birth of Christianity; without it, there would have been no record of the Christ or of his teachings. No contemporary writer or historian mentions him; not until the preaching of the apostles had made his name and doctrines known, does he become a historical character.

The disciples or learners, now changed to apostles or teachers, had the greatest message to proclaim ever given to mankind : "the glad tidings of great joy, which should be to all people."

With the resurrection of the Christ from the dead, as a proof of the spiritual existence of man after the death of the body, the foundation on which all their teaching rested, they proclaimed God, not as Jehovah the Jewish god, but as "our Father," the father and lover of all mankind. They proclaimed a kingdom, or rule, of heaven, here and now, in the heart of every one who loves righteousness.

They proclaimed immortality to be the gift of God to every man who believed in and followed the teachings of the Christ, doing the will of the Father.

The question of the ages, "If a man die, shall he live again?" was for the first time answered by the resurrection of the Christ. With this gospel of the love of God and good-will to man, these apostles of freedom went forth in the glad consciousness of the importance of their mission, into all the world, baptizing in the name of a God of love, a risen Christ, and a helping and enlightening Spirit.

Let us remember that these apostles were human beings, each having and keeping his own individuality. Spiritually they were transformed, as the Christian religion changes every one who embraces it. That transformation is not a change of personality, but a change of character, a change in the object of their lives. They realize that this life is secondary; that the life beyond is the one for which they should strive. And in the case of the apostles, it was not only their work, their duty, an obligation laid upon them by Christ; but it was their joy. They longed to proclaim to the world the good tidings of which they were the chosen messengers; "the good tidings of great joy, which should be to all people;" the tidings of a Saviour, who should save the world from sin (not from the punishment of sin, because sin carries its own punishment, but from sin itself), and from "the wages of sin, which is death."

With the exception of Paul, these apostles had been companions of Christ; had heard his teachings, seen his miracles, caught some of his tenderness, and imbibed of his spirit. They were enlightened by the Holy Ghost, to the extent necessary for them to accomplish the work they had undertaken; and the gift of tongues, a necessary gift at the time, indicated to each one the country in which he was to teach. Their general knowledge outside of their particular work was not enlarged, nor their beliefs on other matters enlightened.

Peter, in his first address to the Jews, on the day of Pentecost, gives, in a few words, the true apostles' creed. He says, —

"Jesus of Nazareth, a man approved of God unto you by mighty works and wonders and signs, which God did in the midst of you, even as you yourselves know; him, being delivered up by the determinate counsel and foreknowledge of God, ye, by the hands of lawless men, did crucify and slay: whom God raised up, having loosed the pangs of death, because it was not possible that he should be holden by it. . . . *This Jesus did God raise up, whereof we are all witnesses.* Being, therefore, by the right hand of God exalted, and having received of the Father the promise of the Holy Ghost, he hath poured forth this which ye see and hear. Let all the house of Israel therefore know assuredly, that God hath made him both Lord and Christ, this Jesus whom ye crucified."

This confession of faith, or statement of belief, is made by Peter as the representative of all the apostles, and without dissent from any one.

It is noticeable that Peter gives the credit of all Christ's miracles, of his resurrection, of the gift of the Holy Ghost, and of his position, to God. Christ was the instrument, but God the ruling power.

The confession of faith contains a charge against the Jews, of having crucified and slain Jesus of Nazareth, their Messiah.

"Now, when they heard this, they were pricked in their hearts, and said unto Peter and the rest of the apostles, Brethren, what shall we do? And Peter said unto them, Repent ye, and be baptized every one of you, in the name of Jesus Christ, unto the remission of your sins, and ye shall receive the Holy Ghost," or spiritual enlightenment.

Let us carefully examine these requirements. First, a belief in the life, miracles, teachings, death, and resurrection of the man Jesus of Nazareth. Second, repentance. From what? From the sin they had been convicted of, namely, being accessory to the murder of Jesus Christ, who they were now convinced was their Messiah, promised of old. And they were now called upon to repent of that sin, and acknowledge their new belief in Jesus as the Christ. Third, the public act of baptism, a rite familiar to them, and signifying the washing-away of old beliefs, previous to the adoption of new; and this repentance and acknowledgment must be public; upon doing this their sins should be remitted, or forgiven, and they should receive the enlightenment of the Holy Spirit. And the record states, "and there were added unto them in that day about three thousand souls; and they *continued* steadfastly in the apostles' teaching and fellowship, in the breaking of bread, and prayers."

In this first work of the apostles, the Jews acknowledged the truth of the statement respecting Jesus, and the call of Jesus is repeated: Repent. We find that they were called to repent of the sins of which they were aware. No claim is made of the universal sinfulness of man through the fall of Adam; total depravity was unknown; nor was Christ's death mentioned as an atonement for the sins of mankind. Christ is spoken of as a man, and even the doctrines of Christ were unmentioned. The only creed subscribed to by these converts was the assent given to the apostles' creed mentioned, by their acceptance of the rite of baptism.

All, then, that these first Christians found required of them, was to acknowledge Jesus as the Christ, that he died and rose again, repent of their sins, and give public notice of their new belief by the outward act of baptism.

When Philip joined the eunuch of Queen Candace, and the eunuch inquired of Philip respecting the prophecies, "Philip opened his mouth, and beginning from this scripture preached unto him Jesus. And as they went on their way, they came unto a certain water, and the eunuch said, Behold, here is water; what doth hinder me to be baptized? And he baptized him; and the eunuch went on his way rejoicing."

He preached unto him Jesus, nothing else; no tales of Adam and Eve, and the Devil, and the fall of man; no total depravity, no five points of Calvinism, — simply Jesus.

Paul and Silas at Macedonia, in answer to the jailer's question, "What must I do to be saved?" answer, "Believe on the Lord Jesus, and thou shalt be saved, thou and thy house. And they spake the word of the Lord unto him, with all that were in his house. And he took them the same hour of the night, and washed their stripes; and was baptized, he and all his, immediately."

To believe in the Lord Jesus, we find, was to

believe in something more than a name or an existence: they spake the *word* of the Lord unto them; and their baptism was an acknowledgment of belief, and an agreement to live in accordance with the teachings of Christ.

At Thessalonica, "Paul, as his custom was, went in unto them, and for three sabbath days reasoned with them from the Scriptures, opening and alleging that it behoved the Christ to suffer, and to rise again from the dead; and that this Jesus, whom, said he, I proclaim unto you, is the Christ."

Christ's work, we have stated, was initiatory. It was now the duty of his disciples to spread abroad the "good tidings of great joy which should be to all people;" and the cross, the emblem of his death and resurrection, was the foundation of their teaching. Christ and him crucified was their subject.

"Greater things than these shall ye do," said Christ to his disciples. To them was given the work which he had inaugurated. His claim of being instructed by God, that he delivered only what he had received of him, that he had been so enlightened by the Holy Spirit, that what he taught was with the certainty, the authority, of knowledge, was now proved by his resurrection from the dead. The great object of his death, which was to prove the existence of the spirit, the soul, the man himself, after the death of the body, was complete and unquestioned. And upon the fact of the resurrection of Christ from the dead, the apostles founded all their teaching; they refer to it continually, as the foundation of their faith, the rock on which the whole superstructure rests.

The event of greatest significance in the life of Christ, and of the greatest importance to mankind, was not his baptism, not his crucifixion and death, but his resurrection from the dead. While his crucifixion and death was the seal of his ministry, the completion of his work, his resurrection was the commencement of his gospel of good tidings.

Christ's life and teachings, his revelations of God, of man, of their relationship, of the kingdom of heaven, and of the future life, were all seeds sown which should bear fruit in the teachings of his disciples.

What could give life to his teachings? What could induce his disciples to go forth and promulgate this doctrine of the kingdom of heaven, and of eternal life, which had been the prominent points in his teaching? Nothing, apparently, but what did take place. Christ's resurrection from the dead was the only thing which could give life and vitality to his doctrines.

We have no account of what he taught after his resurrection. It is evident that the event itself, and what his disciples learned from him, led to an entire change in their views and purposes. His former sayings received new significance; and the enlightenment of the Holy Spirit aided them in understanding his teachings, and in giving to these ignorant and timid disciples courage to go into all the world, preaching the good tidings of the resurrection and eternal life.

German critical writers claim that Jesus of Nazareth taught nothing new; that he merely concentrated and put into a new form old truths, thus giving them new life; that he usurped the title of the Christ, which he knew did not belong to him, and thereafter lived a life of deceit; in short, that this teacher of righteousness, whose precepts reach the springs of action in the heart, was himself a daily violater of the truth; that his disciples followed his example, and falsified the records of his life; and that the apostles, including Paul, did the same in their writings.

When we put into a short sentence the result of their criticisms, their utter inconsistency contradicts their foul assertions.

Except in a few scattered sentences in the Hebrew Scriptures, where, before the Christ, can we find taught the Fatherhood of God, and the brotherhood of man? Who *taught* any thing of the kind? Who *ever* taught the spiritual kingdom of heaven? Who taught of the life eternal, and of the way for man to obtain that great gift of God? Who but the Christ? Are these old truths put into a new form? If so, where can these old truths be found?

Did Jesus of Nazareth usurp a title which did not belong to him?

In the Four Gospels, we have the picture of an exceptional and perfect man; in all points the portrait is complete. Painted by four different artists, each, in all material points, has given us the same picture. Each, however, gives touches here and there, according to his own individuality, which, being brought together, make one complete whole. What can be added to the portrait to make it more complete? or what can we take from it that will improve it?

How beautiful! how grand! how majestic! how sweet! how meek! how humble! What power! what determination! what courage! what purity! what truth! what love! what compassion! what fortitude! what sorrow!

In all history, where is another character that stands out so clear, so full, so well proportioned, so distinct, so complete? And what a life, from beginning to end! each step depending on the preceding; the advance regular, steady, majestic, to its culmination.

Who in those days could have imagined such a person, could have delineated such a life, or enunciated such doctrines? And how impossible for four men each to have falsely drawn the same character! The fact that we have such a record, is proof positive that such a life was lived, and such doctrines were taught. To have imagined such a being, such a life, and such doctrines, was simply impossible; they were out of the power of man to conceive.

There is no accounting for the doctrines, except that they came from God, and were delivered to the human race by a man authorized and commissioned by God so to do. No man, unless he speaks as God's messenger, and by his authority, can open unto us the kingdom of heaven, or show us the way to life eternal. Must not such a man have been the Christ?

Can the man who uttered the Sermon on the Mount, who claimed to be the way, the truth, and the life, be a deceiver, a falsifier? By their fruits ye shall know them. The fruits of the teachings of the Christ are a knowledge of spiritual things, which no man had before; namely, the love and Fatherhood of God; the brotherhood of man; the kingdom of heaven begun on earth; the eternal life, and the way to obtain the same. These are the fruits. Judge ye of the tree. Is it good, or bad? Can a corrupt tree bring forth good fruit?

THE SECOND COMING OF THE CHRIST.

"When they therefore were come together, they asked of him, saying: Lord, wilt thou at this time restore again the kingdom to Israel? And he said unto them, It is not for you to know the times or the seasons, which the Father hath put in his own power; but ye shall receive power after that the Holy Ghost is come upon you; and ye shall be witnesses unto me, both in Jerusalem, and in all Judæa, and in Samaria, and unto the uttermost parts of the earth. And when he had spoken these things, while they beheld, he was taken up; and a cloud received him out of their sight. And while they looked steadfastly toward heaven as he went up, behold two men stood by them in white apparel, which also said, Ye men of Galilee, why stand ye gazing up into heaven? This same Jesus which is taken up from you into heaven shall so come in like manner as ye have seen him go into heaven." (Acts i. 6–11.)

It is evident that the apostles believed and taught the second coming of Christ. Some among them believed that at his second coming he would "establish again the kingdom of Israel." The

Christ, as they believed, was to reign on earth; and why should he come again, unless to establish his kingdom and commence his reign? They expected this second coming would be early; it was imminent; and they called on the disciples to "abide in him, that, when he shall appear, we may have confidence, and not be ashamed before him at his coming." (1 John ii. 28.)

Paul speaks of the Christians at Corinth, as "waiting for the coming of our Lord Jesus Christ." In his first Epistle to the Thessalonians, he says: "I pray God, your whole spirit and soul and body be preserved blameless unto the coming of our Lord Jesus Christ." In his second Epistle, he beseeches them "by the coming of our Lord Jesus Christ."

James exhorts the Christians to "be patient, therefore, brethren, unto the coming of the Lord. . . . Stablish your hearts, for the coming of the Lord draweth nigh."

Paul's belief in the second coming was different in its nature from that of the other apostles. In his first Epistle to the Thessalonians, he states it in these words: "But I would not have you to be ignorant, brethren, concerning them which are asleep, that ye sorrow not, even as others which have no hope. For if we believe that Jesus died and rose again, even so them also which sleep in

Jesus will God bring with him. For this we say unto you by the word of the Lord: that we, which are alive and remain unto the coming of the Lord, shall not prevent them which are asleep; for the Lord himself shall descend from heaven with a shout, with the voice of the archangel, and with the trumpet of God; and the dead in Christ shall rise first; then we which are alive and remain shall be caught up together with them in the clouds, to meet the Lord in the air; and so shall we ever be with the Lord."

This belief in the second appearance of Christ is apparent in their preaching; they expected it to take place in that generation, and this belief was built apparently on the words of Christ. He frequently spoke of his coming again. "The Son of man shall come in the glory of his Father." He "cometh at such an hour as ye think not."

In speaking of John, he says, "If I will that he tarry till I come, what is that to you?" He says, "In an hour that ye think not, the Son of man cometh." "Watch therefore, for ye know not on what day your Lord cometh." "Watch therefore, for ye know not the day, nor the hour." "Verily, I say unto you, There be some standing here, which shall not taste of death, till they see the Son of man coming in his kingdom."

Paul writes to the Thessalonians, "For yourselves know perfectly, that the day of the Lord so cometh as a thief in the night."

The whole import of these words is, that he will come again, and that soon; yet the apostles and Christians of that day, and even down to the present time, have waited in vain for his coming in person. Then, what is meant by the words of the Christ? Were his words untrue? Did he promise what he was unable to perform? Are we still to await his coming, or has he come?

It is the belief of many Christians, that he is yet to come, and that the time draws nigh. But how, and with what body, shall he come? Shall he appear in Jerusalem? In Rome? In England? In America? Who in these sceptical days will vouch for him, and who will believe? Shall he be a Jew? What Christian would acknowledge him? Shall he come a German, a Frenchman, an Englishman, an American? Shall he be a carpenter, a merchant, a mechanic, a scholar? Shall he be born again in the flesh, and grow up from a child to manhood among you without recognition until touched by the enlightening power of the Spirit? Even then who will receive him? Or shall he, as Paul believed, "descend from heaven with a shout, with the voice of the archangel, and with the trump of God"? And if he should thus appear, unless the occasion should be the final day of earth, except those who saw it, who would believe the tale?

The repeated statements of the Christ are that he should come in that generation; and the angels at his ascension say that he should come in the same quiet way in which he ascended, — he "shall so come in like manner as ye have seen him go into heaven." As a spiritual body, spiritually.

All these promises were fulfilled, both in the time and in the circumstances under which they were promised; and they are still in process, and will so continue until the end of the world.

Christ's second coming was to be with power, but quietly, even as he ascended into heaven, without noise or violence. It was to come as a thief in the night, without observation, at such an hour as ye think not of; and in that generation, some of those standing around him should see that day.

They did see that day. All the conditions were fulfilled in the result of Peter's preaching on the Day of Pentecost, when "about three thousand" acknowledged their belief in Jesus as the Christ; a larger number of disciples, probably, than Christ had in the whole course of his first coming. The day came with power; it came quietly, without noise or violence; and in that generation. Even the apostles did not recognize it; it came without observation; it was the dawn of a glorious day, continued and enlarged in the increasing number of believers; a day that under all circumstances, and against all impediments, has continued to grow brighter and brighter, and more and more glorious, and will so continue until "the kingdoms of this world are become the kingdoms of our Lord and of his Christ."

So, too, his promises, that where two or three are met together in his name, there he is in the midst of them, and the promise to be with them alway, even unto the end of the world, are daily and hourly fulfilled. In all Christian countries, and in all meetings of Christians, everywhere, Christ is with them in their thought and conversation. The books, the newspapers, the literature of Christian countries, directly and indirectly, speak of him; his influence surrounds us as an atmosphere; he permeates our thoughts and actions, consciously or unconsciously. Two or three cannot meet together in his name, but he is in the midst of them, in the influence of his life, his teachings and death, and, above all, in his resurrection. Not only in God do we live and move and have our being, but in the Christ we live and move and have our being as Christians. He is our life. His personal re-appearance we can see is impossible, or, if possible, would be without effect; he would again be despised and rejected of men. Spiritually he comes again in the holy lives and conversations of his true disciples, and wherever and whenever his gospel is made known. His real material second coming is in the re-promulgation of his revelation, stripped of the incrustation of hatred, superstition, bigotry, and dogma, which fifteen hundred years of spiritual ignorance have cumulated upon it.

THE CHRIST AN ENIGMA.

Throughout the New Testament, we see the constant non-conceptions or the misconceptions of the Christ's teachings, not only by the Jews generally, but also by his disciples. Jesus spake to them in the language of the Spirit, which to them, until their spiritual enlightenment, was unintelligible. Their idea of the "kingdom of God," or the "kingdom of heaven," was earthly; his was spiritual. Their idea of God was as Jehovah, their national deity; his was as the Father of the whole human race. They believed in their God as a person, like unto a man, but more powerful. The Christ proclaimed him to be a spirit. They worshipped their God in burnt offerings of animals, and fragrant woods and spices. The Christ taught that God should be worshipped in spirit and truth.

The Jews believed that Abraham had talked familiarly with God, and had even argued with him to save the doomed cities; and that Jacob had wrestled all day with God. This belief had led them to look upon Abraham, Isaac, and Jacob as men above the common type, and, for that reason, the favored of God. Moses was not so highly favored: he was permitted to see only his "hinder part" as he passed by.

This personality of Jehovah was so strongly implanted, that the statement of the Christ — that God is a spirit — passed unheeded.

When the Christ spoke of God as our Father, the idea was incomprehensible even to the disciples. We see the dazed way in which they say to him, "Show us the Father, and it sufficeth us." Who or what the Father was, they did not yet comprehend; and Jesus' answer to this request must have still more puzzled them.

It was the same in his frequent conversations with the Jews. They believed in Jehovah, and that his son, the conquering Messiah, would come to earth; but they never thought of calling themselves sons of Jehovah. The thought even was sacrilege. They had Abraham for their father; that was distinction enough. The terms "my Father," "your Father," were so distasteful to the Jews, that the Christ often changed them to "the Father," as less offensive, more especially in his frequent conversations with the priests and scribes at Jerusalem; but without effect. The Jewish mind could not get beyond Jehovah; he was their God, and the Christ would be his son; and he would come with such evidences of power and might, and such credentials, as could not be mistaken. As for this Jesus of Nazareth, who pretended to be the Messiah, all knew of his parentage, and whence he came. What were his miracles, compared with those which would accompany the appearance of the real Christ, the son of the almighty Jehovah? The claim of Jesus was preposterous and blasphemous.

With these opposite ideas and habits of thought, the Christ's claims and teachings were enigmas to both his disciples and the Jews. He was speaking for the future instruction of his disciples in all ages; until they obtain the spiritual key, none can understand him.

See his conversation with Nicodemus upon being born again. His claim, "No man hath ascended *up* into heaven, but he that came down *from* heaven, even the Son of man which is *in* heaven," to them was a paradox. The "living water" that he could give the woman of Samaria, which should be "a well of water springing up into everlasting life," to her was still a myth.

The daring claim made, that he was the Son of Jehovah; the statement that "my Father worketh hitherto, and I work;" and the long argument he presents to substantiate his claim as he spake now of Jehovah, and now of the Father, — must have greatly puzzled them.

So, too, in Capernaum he says, "I am the living bread which came down from heaven. If any man eat of this bread, he shall live forever; and the bread I will give is my flesh, which I will give for the life of the world." Is it any wonder that "the Jews therefore strove among themselves, saying, How can this man give us his flesh to eat? And many of his disciples said, This is an hard saying; who can hear it?" And the record states, "From that time many of his disciples went back, and walked no more with him."

At another time, he says, "My doctrine is not mine, but his that sent me. If any man shall do his will, he shall know of the doctrine, whether it be of God, or whether I speak of myself." His sayings so puzzled the people, that they said, "Thou hast a devil." Again he cries unto them, "He that believeth on me, . . . out of his belly shall flow rivers of living water." He calls himself "the light of the world; he that followeth me shall not walk in darkness, but shall have the light of life." He says, "The Father that sent me beareth witness of me. Then said they unto him, Where is thy Father?" To this query he vouchsafes no answer but the assertion, "Ye neither know me, nor my Father."

He holds a long argument with the Jews, almost acrimonious in its character, every statement of which would to them be a riddle. "I go my way; and ye shall seek me, and shall die in your sins. Whither I go, ye cannot come." Then said the Jews, Will he kill himself? He goes on: "Ye are from beneath; I am from above. Ye are of this world; I am not of this world. . . . If ye believe not that I am he, ye shall die in your sins. They say unto him, Who art thou? Jesus saith unto them, Even the same that I said unto you from the beginning." He further says, "I speak that which I have seen with my Father, and ye do that which ye have seen with your father. . . . Ye are of your father the devil, and the lusts of your father ye will do. . . . He that is of God heareth God's words; ye therefore hear them not, because ye are not of God. Then answered the Jews, and said unto him, Say we not well, that thou art a Samaritan, and hast a devil?" He then proceeds, changing the subject: "If a man keep my saying, he shall never see death." The Jews answer, "Now we know that thou hast a devil. Abraham is dead, and the prophets. . . .

Art thou greater than our father Abraham, which is dead? and the prophets are dead. Whom makest thou thyself? Jesus answered, It is my Father that honoreth me; of whom ye say that he is your God; yet ye have not known him; but I know him, and if I should say I know him not, I shall be a liar like unto you. . . . Your father Abraham rejoiced to see my day, and he saw it, and was glad. Then said the Jews unto him, Thou art not yet fifty years old, and hast thou seen Abraham? Jesus said unto them, Verily, verily, I say unto you, Before Abraham was, I am;" a statement in their view perfectly astounding.

The Christ at another time utters this paradox: "For judgment I am come into this world; that they which see not, might see; and that they which see might be made blind. And some of the Pharisees which were with him heard these words, and said unto him, Are we blind also? Jesus said unto them, If ye were blind, ye should have no sin; but now ye say, We see; therefore your sin remaineth." He then likens himself to the Good Shepherd, and claims to have the power "of laying down his life, and of taking it again." And "many of them said, He hath a devil, and is mad." Again, he claims the power of giving eternal life to those who believe on him; and that he and his Father were one. "Then the Jews took up stones to stone him." Again, speaking of his death, Jesus says, "And I, if I be lifted up from the earth, will draw all men unto me. The people answered him, We have heard, out of the law, that Christ abideth forever; and how sayest thou, The Son of man must be lifted up? Who is this Son of man?" We see their utter want of conception of his teachings. This question, like many others, he does not answer; but advises them to walk in the light.

We see all through, that his disciples understood him as little as did the Jews. In his last talk with them, he says, "A little while, and ye shall not see me; and again a little while, and ye shall see me; because I go to my Father;" and his disciples say, "What is this that he saith, a little while? we cannot tell what he saith." He finally tells them, however, "These things have I spoken to you in proverbs; but the time cometh when I shall no more speak to you in proverbs, but I shall show you plainly of the Father."

THE HOLY SPIRIT IN THE NINETEENTH CENTURY.

This enlightening and spiritual power and influence, known to us as the Holy Spirit, has been exhibited in various ways, at different periods of the world's history, in accordance with the necessities of the times and occasions, — by

Moses, in exhibitions of its power over nature's laws in certain directions; by Joshua, and occasionally by others of the Hebrew heroes and soldiers, and by Elijah and Elisha, in other directions; by the prophets, in the revelation of future events, and in their higher and purer revelations of God; and by the Christ, in his full revelation of the Deity, the good tidings of great joy.

This Holy Spirit was also given in a modified form to the apostles. Dull and unspiritual as they were as disciples, — learners, — after the Christ's resurrection, he no longer addressed them "in proverbs," but, as he had promised, spake to them "plainly of the Father." After his ascension, they received the gift of the Holy Spirit. Their minds having been enlightened by the Christ respecting the object and character of his mission, they could go back in thought to his teachings; and, under the new light breaking in upon them, the meaning and intent of his words dawned upon them. What was before dark and obscure became bright with the light of the Spirit. Their minds were enlarged by this spiritual birth; and, as the extent and grandeur of their mission grew upon them, they became new men, filled with the Holy Ghost and with power.

Men have looked upon this power, as its results have been recorded in the Bible, as if it were a strange and exceptional power; something used in Bible times, for particular purposes, but lost and unknown to man at the present time. This is a mistake. At no time since the world began (unless in early Aryan days) has this spiritual power been so fully developed and so freely bestowed as in this nineteenth century, especially during the past fifty years. In that time, man, by the aid of this spiritual power, has boldly grasped many natural laws, and forced them to obey his will. What were the so-called miracles of Moses, to the miracles created by the before-hidden powers of steam and electricity? What the power wielded by Joshua, Elijah, and Elisha, to those exhibited on every railroad, steamship, and factory? The power exerted by mind over matter is everywhere seen and acknowledged. Let us give the proper name to it, and say, the power of the spiritual over the natural. This power was known to, and was acknowledged by, the early Aryas. Let us do the same.

The idea that the apostles, because of their companionship with Jesus, were specially enlightened and pre-eminently fitted to teach the gospel of good tidings, is false. For their day and generation, they were well fitted, because they were the only ones that had, and could impart, the good news; but to-day not a minister of the gospel but has better means and opportunities of judging of the teachings of the Christ, than had any one of the apostles.

The Spirit enlarges not only the soul, that is, the religious part of our nature, but it also expands the intellect. We have four different sources of knowledge respecting the teachings of the Christ. They together give us a more complete record than had either of the apostles of his own personal knowledge. Our whole religious natures have been enlarged, and our spiritual training enables us to recognize more fully than did the apostles the spiritual character and purpose of his mission.

In the dark days of spiritual death, men, in their ignorance and superstition passing by and ignoring the teachings of the author and finisher of our faith, formulated creeds and theologies based upon misconceptions and wilful misconstructions of portions of the Hebrew scriptures, modified or enlarged by utterances of one or other of the apostles; thus making the kingdom of God of none effect by their traditions.

To-day the missionary who will go forth in the name and as the disciple of his Master, to preach the simple faith of the Christ, will go better prepared and equipped, mentally and spiritually, to spread the gospel of good tidings, than were the apostles of old for the work before them; and they will promulgate a doctrine nearly as little known in Christian countries, so called, as it is in heathen lands.

Ye so-called Christians, awake from your lethargy and sin. Dig up the discarded teachings of your Christ. Cleanse them from the pollutions and stains of fifteen hundred years of ignorance, bigotry, superstition, and crime; and come forth as believers in the Christ in whose name you claim to live, and spread abroad in the names of a loving Father, of an anointed and living Christ, and an ever-present and enlightening Holy Spirit, the good tidings of the kingdom of heaven, immortal life, and the way. Thus shall the Christ again appear; and his second coming shall be with greater power, and more glorious, than the first.

FALSE CHRISTIANITY.

In the course of a few hundred years after his death, a great change had taken place in the simple religion of the Christ. Adopted as the national religion of Rome, it took on forms and ceremonies incompatible with the teachings of its founder. It grew into a religious tyranny, claiming authority over the conscience of man in this world, and power over his future well-being in the world to come.

The monotheism taught by the Christ gradually changed; the Christ himself was robbed of his humanity, and was clothed by the priestly hierarchy with the powers of the Deity. The holy spirit of God was personified; and the two, as gods, were added to the being of the Deity, the three being made one godhead; the Deity being thus transformed into a three-one, a triune God, a contradiction of terms which the mind of man cannot comprehend, whose incomprehensibility is hidden under the mask of a "holy mystery."

This change in the constitution and being of the Infinite was accompanied by a corresponding change in man's idēa of God; and the "Father" was hidden from view, by the greater prominence given to the Son as the lover and Saviour of mankind.

In the breaking-up of the great Roman Empire, and the continuous wars which for hundreds of years convulsed Europe and Western Asia, the Christian religion rapidly declined, and ignorance and superstition took its place. These wars, with the frequent irruptions of the Goths, Vandals, and other Northern hordes, and the inroads of the Huns, with the later uprising and spread of the Saracenic and Arabian power, in the course of a thousand years almost entirely destroyed the Christian religion; and the Aryan race, for the third time, slept the sleep of ignorance.

During this time the Church, as it was called, concentrated its power, and enlarged its scope. Working upon the superstitions of men, in the general ignorance which prevailed, it wielded a power over their lives and consciences before unknown. Outside of the monasteries and the dignitaries of the Christian Church, there were few, even of the nobles, who could read or write; many of the priests were equally ignorant with the people. The simple teachings of the Christ had, even in its earlier days, been contaminated by the additions of heathen rites and ceremonies, and hidden by numerous theological tests and requirements; to these had now been added the debasing use of power obtained over the fears and superstitions of men, by bold claims of spiritual control over their souls, by reason of apostolic descent from the Apostle Peter, to whom, it was claimed, the keys of heaven were intrusted by the Christ, and through which descent, the Pope, or highest officer of the Church, had obtained the authority of deciding the future destiny of the soul, in accordance with his individual will.

This power was not only wielded by the Pope, but the most ignorant priest of the time claimed by reason of his office, and the power bestowed upon him by the Pope, the same control over the future of the nominal Christians about him.

In this long period of intellectual and spiritual decline in Europe, many of the arts and sciences of Aryan civilization were lost. The nations declined into barbarism, but little above that of savages; violence and crime took the place of law and order; every man's hand was against his neighbors, and might made right.

In the mean time Asia advanced rapidly in civilization and wealth. Arabia became the depository of the learning and knowledge of the world; and for the second time the Semite received the Aryan civilization, which it retained for five or six hundred years, when it was again placed in the hands of the Aryas.

It was during this, a period well called the "dark ages," that there arose in Europe a false Christianity: a theology that cannot be equalled in any heathen country in the superstitious ferocity of its teachings, in the inhumanity of the God of its worship, and in the savage cruelty of the God it fears, but pretends not to worship.

Believing the Bible to be one book written by authority of God, and all parts of equal weight and value, they took from the initial book of the worn-out and cast-away Hebrew Scriptures an Eastern symbolical story of the spiritual advance of Adam and Eve. The Deity had planted a garden in Eden, in which he placed every thing for the use and pleasure of man, at the same time placing in one corner thereof two remarkable trees. The fruit of one would give unto the eater spiritual glory; the fruit of the other would confer eternal youth.

In this garden God placed Adam and Eve to take care of, and eat, the fruit thereof.

For a time these trees were unseen; but when noticed, Adam and Eve were afraid to partake of the fruit, for fear they were poisonous. At this point of the story, Wisdom appears in the form of a serpent, and advises Eve to eat of the fruit of the tree of knowledge, saying to her that she need not be afraid; that the fruit was not poisonous, and would not injure her: on the contrary, it would be exhilarating, healthy, invigorating, and strengthening to the body, would enlighten the understanding, and give clear mental vision.

Thus advised, tempted by the beauty of the fruit and by her desire to obtain greater knowledge, she, with her husband, partook of the fruit, with the result foretold by Wisdom. Their spiritual eyes were opened. They saw that many of their former practices, under the new light they had received, were evil; and conscience called upon them to reform and do better. The continual eating of the fruit gave them a knowledge of better ways; and now, too, they see the tree of eternal youth, and long to partake thereof, but are prevented from so doing except under certain conditions imposed by the Deity. For what they have already done in partaking of the fruit of the tree of knowledge, God speaks in approbation, and likens them to himself in their ability to choose between good and evil. He will not permit them to partake of the fruit of the tree of life, except as the reward for services rendered.

This beautiful little Eastern apologue fell into the hands of men without imagination, and ignorant of Oriental symbolism; and, instead of looking for its hidden meaning, they seized upon it as a matter of fact; perverted it from its plain teaching by changing the serpent from a symbol of wisdom into Satan, a god of evil; made the fruit of the tree of knowledge poisonous; ignored the fact that it was recorded as giving the knowledge of *good* as well as evil, and made the results of eating of it as wholly evil, — a source of degradation and sin; turned the curse of the earth for *Adam's sake, his benefit,* into a curse upon Adam himself; ignored the praise of God, and shut out the tree of eternal youth to all mankind.

In addition, they claimed that Adam, in eating of the fruit of the tree of knowledge, had transgressed a law of God; and that, in so doing, he had fallen from a state of innocence into sin; and that this sin of Adam was entailed as a disease on all his race.

This transformation of the symbolical tale of spiritual advance, into a story of degradation, sin, and shame, shutting out man forever from partaking of the fruit of the tree of eternal youth, led to views of the Creator necessarily degrading. Either the Deity, after all his long and careful work in preparing this earth for the use and enjoyment of his children, had unexpectedly come in contact with another god, of whose existence he was not previously aware, who proved to be his superior in power, and who took forcible possession of his children; or, knowing of the existence of this powerful god, he carelessly left Adam and Eve, the children of his love, without warning them of their danger, or teaching them how to escape the peril which threatened them.

Both of these conceptions of God were too belittling, and they advanced a bolder but more cruel hypothesis; namely, that God created Satan as his servant, and the minister of his wrath, at the same time creating hell, filled with eternal fire and innumerable instruments of torture, with devils without number to aid in tormenting his children who had disobeyed, or who should disobey, his will.

This hypothesis they made the basis of a theology the most cruel, the most horrible, ever invented by the imagination of man or devil. In it the Deity is represented as placing Adam and Eve, and all their innocent descendants, forever in the hands of Satan and his imps, to remain forever in torment, because of Adam's sin. What a tremendous punishment for a trivial offence! And this, not as a just punishment for wrongdoing, but to gratify the vengeance and hate of God. What blasphemy!

For four thousand years or more, they claimed this was done; and the Deity continually gave life to children, only that they might be turned over to the tormentors. At the end of that period, the Christ, the Son of God, took compassion on the sufferings of mankind, and earnestly desired to save them from the certain and endless doom that awaited them; and, at his earnest request, the Father consented that he might take upon himself the form and nature of man, and undergo in his person the full punishment for the sins of the world, thereby relieving man from the doom before placed upon him by God. This was done, and the Christ suffered on the cross for the sins of all mankind.

Instead, however, of the sacrifice of the Christ freeing mankind from their sufferings, the only effect was to relieve the few who, born in a country where the sacrifice of the Christ was known, should accept that sacrifice as an atonement for their sins, and thus be saved from the hands of Satan. Thus was the Christ cheated out of the fruits of his sacrifice; and where one is saved by his act, a thousand are plunged into hell through ignorance of the work done by the Christ.

According to this theology, the Deity, instead of being our Father, is made a vengeful and hateful being, too horrible to look at, and withal deceitful in withholding from the Christ the reward for his suffering and pain.

This foul satire on the religion of the Christ, originating in the foul imaginations of men, degraded by ignorance and superstition, received from the Romish Church, and indorsed by the Protestant Church, was formed into a mathematical system by Calvin. In this form it was forced upon man by burning, torture, and death, and became so firmly fixed, that to-day almost the entire Christian body intellectually or superstitiously assent to the theology; while in their hearts thousands disbelieve, and show in their happy lives and conversation their entire disbelief, in this fiendish theology.

The great achievement of false Christianity was the placing of reason under a ban. The triune God was a great mystery, incomprehensible to finite minds, and beyond the power of reason to explain. Christians were, consequently, required to believe it as belonging to the infinite.

It is no wonder that in the dark ages, those days of carnage and murder, of might against right, those days of all manner of iniquity, — that their religion should be of the same nature: it could not be otherwise. It was impossible for the religion of the Christ to live in such blackness of ignorance, superstition, and despair. But, providentially, the record of the Christ's teaching was not lost: in monasteries, the work of pious men saved the records; these we now have, and by them we can judge this detestable religion which for so long a time has falsely born the name of Christian.

As it has always been, the God worshipped by man is a reflex image of himself. In old times, men tried to give shape to the god of their imaginations, in images of wood, stone, or metal; in later times, they have embodied it in dogma and creed.

To-day, every minister holds up to his audience the God of his sect or denomination to be worshipped; and we have the Calvinistic, the Methodist, the Orthodox, the Catholic, the Baptist, and other Gods, each being the same false God of a false Christianity, clad in a different dress, and each claiming the exclusive indorsement of the

Christ; and the individual man, led by men equally as spiritually blind as himself, accepts one of these images as the truthful image of our God and Father revealed by the Christ. These images, which bear the likeness of nothing in heaven above, or in the earth beneath, or in the waters under the earth, are accepted by these deluded men; and thousands to-day worship these mediæval gods in ignorance of their true character.

The general distribution of the Bible in the last two hundred years has greatly enlightened and ameliorated these so-called Christian dogmas. The teachings of the Christ have been received into the hearts of many whose love for humanity was greater than was the love of their theological god; their hearts have swelled with the desire to alleviate suffering; and they have exerted themselves for the salvation of men from the eternal torture they believed awaited them. Cruel and revengeful laws have been annulled; the slave has been made free; prisons have been governed with more humanity; hospitals, homes for the poor, and institutions of charity, have arisen under this influence.

Gradually the belief in the fatherhood and love of God, and the brotherhood of man, is entering into the heart, and is becoming embodied in the lives of men; and the glorious evangel of the

Christ, in all its beauty and loveliness, is beginning to dawn; and mankind are making ready to break the chains of bigotry and superstition which have so long bound them, and are ready to leap forward into the glad life and freedom of the kingdom of God.

LOYALTY TO GOD.

The Christ, in announcing the law of love to God, claims as his due the whole power, energy, and being of man. Love and loyalty are almost synonymous terms. A man shows his love for his country by his willingness to suffer, and, if needs be, die for it, as has been shown by hundreds of thousands, in all ages and countries. So Christianity has its roll of hundreds of thousands who have shown their love and loyalty by suffering and death. While the emblem of loyalty, in the one case, was the flag of their country, the emblem in the other case, for both Catholic and Protestant, was the same cross of the Christ. That is the symbol which unites all Christian sects and denominations. In both of these cases, they gave the whole heart, soul, mind, and strength, to the accomplishment of their object, in loyalty to their country or their God.

This loyalty God requires at all times. "Thou shalt have no other gods before me," he says. You may have other gods, but they shall be secondary, subsidiary. To the Deity belongs the first place; none shall be superior to or preferred before him. If any other god is given the preference, He leaves entirely, and cannot be approached until the offending god has been removed. He will not listen to the prayers, or answer the requests, of those who dethrone him from his supreme place in their heart and lives. To those who are loyal to him, he is ever present, upholding and supporting them in all circumstances, and comforting them under all trials and afflictions. For instance:—

One makes AMBITION his god; working for political power and fame, using every means to advance his personal popularity, giving his life and strength to that one object, without one thought of the God who made him, whose child he is, who gave him his exceptional powers to be used for the benefit of his fellow-men, instead of using them for his own base and selfish ends. These powers used in subjection to, and under the guidance of, the Deity, for the well-being of man, would have made the possessor a benefactor of his race; but, used for selfish ends, they become a burden and a snare to their possessor.

Others make WEALTH their god, unmindful of their obligations to the God who gave them being. They work day and night; use every means, fair or foul, to accomplish their selfish ends, without thought of or care for the rights of others. They grasp every thing within their reach, until finally they have attained their ends; they have wealth in abundance, but they are unable to enjoy it. They have become the slaves of the god of their worship; and he requires of them unceasing labor, that they may retain the wealth so basely accumulated, and they find no rest. In thus spending their lives, they have lost their own souls; when they think they can begin to enjoy their ill-gotten gains, they are called upon to give them up, and they pass to their place without a single coin of the realm to carry with them. Poor, poor indeed, is such a man, without God or heaven. Such is the terrible state of the man who makes wealth his god.

When he can no longer use it himself, he sometimes attempts to make terms with the Deity by dedicating a portion to charitable purposes; forgetting that the wealth is not his own, but held by him simply as trustee or almoner of the Deity. "The silver and the gold are mine, saith the Lord." If he wishes to do good with it, let him dispose of it while living, and thereby, perhaps, gain the true coin of the realm, namely, love to God and man, the only coin man can take with him to the world beyond.

A common source of trouble, and perhaps the most pardonable, is the deification of CHILDREN. Parents receiving a child from God forget the hand that gave it, and place their affections entirely on the child. They watch over it with jealous care; nothing is too good for it, and nothing must be denied it. The father works for it, the mother spends for it. As it grows, it becomes a tyrant ruling over both, and they become its willing slaves. Should it be taken away, then is their desolation complete. They have put the child in the place of God, and now in their troubles they cannot find him; he has left them to their god, and he is dead, and they are comfortless.

Others, again, make the SENSES their god. They are in the enjoyment of exuberant health. They enjoy the beauties of nature, the sea, mountain, and forest; to ride, to walk, is happiness. They enjoy the beauty and fragrance of the flowers; the fruits in their season delight their taste; the birds make melody in their ears, and they revel in creature enjoyments. In their young manhood, every thing is delightful. God has filled the earth with loveliness, for the use and pleasure of his children. Forgetting the Author and Giver of these good things, they make these and other sensual pleasures the object of their lives, and thus become the slaves of their senses. Animal pleasures soon pall; without God there is no such thing as happiness; and man seeks in new and forbidden paths some new source of delight; and thus palled, satiated, and dead to all high aims, he finally grovels in the dead waste of drunkenness and despair, a victim to the god of the senses.

One of the saddest, and, owing to the generally high social standing of the votaries, perhaps the most dangerous in its influence on others, is the god of the INTELLECT. We find scientists, professors in our colleges and institutions of learning, physicians, and even those claiming to be ministers of the gospel, who have exalted the intellect to the position of supreme god; who, in bowing down and worshipping this god of the intellect, have dwarfed their whole being. Unable to find God by their scientific tests, or measure him with their yard-sticks, they almost doubt his existence; they cannot hear, see, touch, taste, or smell him; and, bewildered, they doubt. Their reason tells them there must be a first cause for what they see around them, but it does not give them light. The things of the spirit are spiritually discerned; the intellect cannot reach so high. These votaries of the intellect grope in darkness and blindness for a first cause, and we see them carried away by every fresh intellectual craze, and seeking in vain for rest.

In these instances, we see the danger of placing any other god in the place of the Supreme Being, whose children we are, and who demands the first place in our affections. His command is essential for our welfare, and we cannot disobey without great injury to ourselves.

All these gods, as subsidiary to the Supreme God, are deities of beneficence, and, under the guidance of Omnipotence, shower down blessings on the heads of their votaries; but, elected to the supreme place, they become veritable demons; their blessings are turned into curses, and their votaries become their degraded and miserable slaves.

THE SECOND GARDEN OF EDEN.

For four thousand years after the deluge, the Aryas again slept the sleep of animal existence, having fallen from the former position so far, that they were but little in advance of their earlier brothers when they threw off their nomadic habits and life. Again they entered the Garden of Eden, which was not now the peninsula of Hindostan, but the world; and again were they required " to dress it and to keep it."

In the persons of the Persians, the Greeks, and the Romans, they again adopted civilization, and gradually took up the arts and sciences which they had so long before laid down.

Jesus, the Christ, revealed to them for the second time the tree of knowledge, and showed unto them the tree of life. Again did they partake of the fruit of the tree of knowledge. God and his laws were again made known to them, and they were enabled to judge between good and evil; and again they recognized the tree of life, and saw clearly the way.

Again the Aryan learned that the serpent of temptation must be placed under his feet, that his animal instincts must be placed in subjection, and used for the happiness of man and the glory of God the Father.

Again God rescued the woman from the degradation of the animal, and placed her in the arms of man as a helpmeet for him, and waits to hear for the second time the acknowledgment of Adam, that woman, whom he has honored by choosing her as the transmitter of his life, the mother and teacher of all his children, is "the mother of all living."

Through the Christ they have again obtained a knowledge of a life beyond, of an immortality for which they long, and which makes the loveliness and grandeur of this present world grow dim before the glories of the eternal world in view.

This tree of life is still guarded from seizure by the flaming sword of God's requirements; it is still in his hands, and both God and Christ unite in showing unto man that the only way to obtain its fruit is to do his will.

Again has God taught the Aryas that all men are his children, the objects of his care and love; that, while man is the father of the fleshly body which perishes, he is the Father of the spiritual body which has the power to live forever.

God has for the second time placed in the hands of the Aryan race the destinies of mankind. Again they have passed, or are passing, through the early experiences depicted in the allegory. By observing these they can trace the progress of this their second trial, mark the steps already taken, and those yet in the future. May they take warning, and not follow in the decline and fall of their fathers!

Eighteen hundred years have passed since Jesus the Christ revealed to the Aryan race for the second time the tree of knowledge and the tree of life; yet how few of those calling themselves Christians have partaken freely of the fruit of the tree of knowledge, or seen in all its beauty the tree of life!

God required the Aryas to dress and keep the garden: yet they have allowed it to be overrun with foul and pestiferous weeds, and its paths to be obstructed by filth and *débris*. The foul and baleful tree of false Christianity has grown triumphantly, and almost hid from sight both the tree of the knowledge of good and evil, and the tree of life; its interlacing branches have presented an almost impenetrable barrier; year after year it has ripened, and sent broadcast its poisonous fruits of religious fanaticism, self-righteousness, uncharitableness, intolerance, persecution, and death. The rank weeds of religious hate and animosity have grown up around it, the tangled vines of bigotry and superstition obstruct the way, and the thorny hedges of sect and dogma prevent advance.

Yet every year there have been a few who have pierced through all these obstructions, and obtained the fruit of the tree of the knowledge of good and evil, and have seen in all its beauty and freshness the tree of life; and through them we know the trees are still there, and can be reached by those who are earnest and persevering.

It is the first duty of the Aryas to remove the hedges of sect and dogma, to clear up the tangled vines of bigotry and superstition, eradicate the weeds of religious hate and animosity, and to dig up and destroy utterly the tree of false Christianity, that it may no more bring forth its baleful fruit for the poisoning of the nations. They should also remove and cast out the pestiferous weeds of ignorance, and the filth and *débris* cast from the dry branches of old and dead faiths which obstruct the paths of the garden, that the tree of knowledge may be easily reached, and its fruit freely partaken of, and that the tree of life, and the way thereof, may be seen and recognized of all. Then shall the Aryas be able to go into all the world, proclaiming to all nations the glad evangel of the love and fatherhood of God, the brotherhood of man, the kingdom, law, or government of heaven, the immortal life, and the way to obtain it.

For five hundred years the Aryan race had ruled the civilized world. The Hamite race of Egypt had sunk into its original insignificance. The Semites of the Euphrates Valley had become merged in their conquerors. The Jews alone, of all the inferior white races, still had a national existence. They had accomplished the work for which they had been created as a nation. They had been the instrument in the hands of the Deity to again bring forth his evangel; but they were not to promulgate it. They did not accept, but rejected it, and crucified the man through whom it was revealed. The obligation was not on the Semites, but upon the Aryas, to "till the ground from whence they were taken."

To give to all mankind this evangel now again placed in their hands, is the duty still devolving on the Aryas of to-day. Moved by the doctrine of hate promulgated by Calvin, they have endeavored to save mankind from the eternal damnation of hell. Are they ready to believe that " God is love "? that the love of man for his fellow-man is but the faint reflection of the love that God feels, and has shown in his creation for his children, the offspring of his Spirit, and the objects of his daily care?

Can man believe that his desires to save his brothers and sisters from the tortures of the damned, are immeasurably surpassed by the desire of the Deity to save them from the shame, anguish, and torture of remorse, which will cause the guilty soul to cry out for the rocks to cover him and hide him from his own degradation and sin? Will the Aryan races of to-day promulgate his evangel of love, that all mankind may know and serve and love him; that his will may indeed be done on earth, even as it is in heaven?

Aryas, the full revelation from God our Father is in your hands. What say ye?

THE COMPLETION OF THE SECOND REVELATION, AND THE END OF THE JEWISH NATION.

It is difficult for us, surrounded as we are by Christian influences and habits of thought, to realize the ignorance, barbarism, religious fanaticism and bigotry, the hatreds and passions, of the Jews at the Christian era.

At that time, by their continual intermarriages, they had established a physiognomy and character known and acknowledged by all; which, by the same process, they have continued to the present time; a face and character as distinct in type as are the Chinese.

Let us take the Jews as they are to-day in Europe and Asia; carry them back to their isolated position as a nation in their own land, instead of wanderers in strange lands; add to their present characteristics, the gross ignorance and fanaticism of the time mentioned, and this fanaticism increased by their hatred of heathen nations, and by their belief in the brightness of their own destiny. Even then, we can hardly conceive of the rancor and bitter hate which they felt and showed to their conquerors, and the pride with which they looked down on all other nations.

More especially was this the case with the higher classes; the priests, the scribes, the Pharisees, the rich, the influential and learned. They were proud and arrogant; looking down upon the poorer classes with haughty contempt, and upon all other nations as heathen, worshippers of idols, as people detested by Jehovah, and as doomed sooner or later to become the bondmen and servants of his chosen nation.

This hate was intensified by the expected advent of the Christ, whose special mission was to free them from the detested bonds of the Romans; establish the kingdom of heaven, or rule of Jehovah, upon earth; and place them, as the ruling people, upon a pinnacle of power and glory.

For many years the hope and expectation of a Messiah had reigned in their hearts, and now the time had arrived for the fulfilment of the prophecies. These prophecies they fully believed in their earthly sense, and daily awaited the coming of the promised Messiah with ever-increasing impatience. The Roman yoke galled them the more from their belief in its now short duration; and it led them to frequent outbursts of fnry, accompanied by expressions of disdain and contempt. These ebullitions of feeling, both private and public, called forth the stern and retributive action of the Romans.

With feelings and expectations so excited, we can readily see with what contempt they would look upon the miracles of the Christ, with what impatience and scorn they would hear of his claim to be their Messiah.

What! this poor carpenter's son, a Nazarene, followed by a rabble of the lowest class, fishermen of Galilee, — their Messiah? their king? the conqueror of the Romans? Impossible! Where was his army? Where his mighty acts? Where were the signs of his power? He might have the power of miracle to a small extent; he might be a prophet; he might be a forerunner of the Mighty One: but he their Christ? God forbid! They could not listen with patience to his pretensions.

It was impossible for the Jews, with their high-wrought expectations of military power and glory, of dominion and rule over the whole world, to give up all their long-brooded schemes of revenge, all their dreams of glory, all their ambitious hopes, and listen to this minister of peace and good-will, this preacher of righteousness, this man who taught the forgiveness of enemies, the returning of good for evil, the submission to and patient endurance of wrong. Jesus, the Nazarene, could not and should not be their Christ. The Christ was to live and rule forever; he could not die. They would prove that he was not the Christ, by putting him to death.

In the coming of the Christ, the destiny and

work of the Hebrew nation was completed. It had been created for that purpose alone; that purpose accomplished, the Deity had no further use for it, and the end came. The nation that crucified the Christ could not live.

"He came unto his own, and his own received him not; but as many as received him, to them gave he power to become the sons of God."

THE ESSENTIALS OF CHRISTIANITY.

It is very possible, that in the interval of time between the utterance by the Christ of his teachings, and the recording of them by the apostles, while the most striking and important of them would be firmly impressed on the memory, and be recorded verbatim, other sayings would be varied in their verbal construction, retaining the original meaning only. In the process of translating, the belief of the translator would color his translation, and the careless or intentional changes of the copier make other changes in the record. But, in all essential points, the records coincide.

Leaving out the birth and childhood of Jesus of Nazareth, and taking the record of his manhood as Jesus the Christ, they agree on these points: namely, that the Christ had extraordinary enlightenment and power; that he claimed to be the Christ, and in proof referred unhesitatingly to the miracles he performed as sustaining that claim, and miracles in abundance are testified to by the Evangelists; that as the Christ he had been taught of God, respecting what he should teach to man; that, being so taught, he proclaimed as the words of God, the great and until then unsuspected fact, that God was our Father, and we the children of his love and care; that there was a kingdom of heaven and an eternal life which we might obtain by doing his will.

They also concur in the statements, that this Christ was publicly crucified on the cross; that on the third day he arose from the tomb, and was seen of his disciples and others. This was also testified to by his disciples unanimously.

The essential points of the Christ's teachings are those mentioned above; and the essential points of his life are his crucifixion, and resurrection from the dead.

These things are not only recorded and testified to by the Evangelists, but are also indorsed by all the apostles in their public utterances. They are the substance of the teachings of the apostles, including Paul. These teachings dominate the writings of the New Testament; they are the woof and warp thereof, and cannot be eliminated without the destruction of the whole fabric.

APPENDIX.

EARLY CIVILIZATION IN THE EUPHRATES VALLEY.

OUR previous volume ended with the dispersion of the Aryas occupying the Euphrates Valley, as the result of war with the Turanians. As yet we have no historical records covering the time intervening between that event and the call of Abram. Egyptian history points to two events of moment which we have related. We believe that future researches will bring to light records confirming the truth of the history revealed in the allegory.

In this Appendix we have given extracts from various Assyriologists establishing the fact of an advanced civilization, which must have existed thousands of years previous to the reign of Sargon I., B.C. 3800.

Professor Sayce says, "The Semitic conquest must have been a gradual one. The evidence of language shows, that, when the Semites first came into contact with the civilization of Accad, they were mere desert nomads, dwelling in tents, and wanting even the first elements of culture. These, however, they soon acquired from their neighbors; and, with the trading instinct of their race, quickly made themselves indispensable to the agricultural Accadians. Ur and the other towns on the western bank of the Euphrates were the earliest places in which they settled, but they soon overflowed into the whole plain of Sumir (Shinar)."

The date of the Semitic irruption is unknown; but as a Semitic king, Sargon I., was reigning B.C. 3800, and at that time the Turanian language had become nearly obsolete, it is apparent that the Semites must have made their appearance within two or three hundred years of the departure of the Aryas. Throwing off their wandering habits, they adopted the manners and customs of the Turanians, learning from them the arts and sciences of civilization. Constant increase from others of their race who also adopted a civilized life gradually enlarged their numbers; apparently they intermarried with the Turanians; and eventually, being a superior, they became the ruling, race. The Turanian language gradually died out, and was replaced by the Semitic.

In absorbing the Turanian civilization, knowledge, government, and religion, they also adopted many Turanian civilized, technical, and scientific words and names, — the same thing having been previously done by the Turanians, when they learned of the Aryas their arts and civilization. The Turanians gave to their rulers the title of "shepherds" or "shepherd kings," which title we find was adopted by the Semites.

Professor Sayce, writing of what he calls the " primitive population of Babylonia and Assyria," says, " they belonged to a race which may have been allied to the Turanian or Finno-Tartar. At all events, it spoke an agglutinative language, which has many affinities with those of the Ural-Altaic family. This primitive population was supplanted by the Semites, — the Casdim, or conquerors, of the Bible, — at some unknown period before the second millennium B.C.

"Before the Semitic period, and *before the earliest period of which we have contemporaneous history*, the Accadian character had been classified and arranged. . . . From the earliest period, the literature of Chaldæa was stored in public libraries. According to Brasus, Pantibibla, or 'book town,' was one of the antediluvian cities of Babylonia; and Zisuthros (the Chaldæan Noah) had buried his books at Sippara before the flood." [1]

Not being aware of the existence of the Aryan race in the Euphrates valley previous to the Turanian occupancy, these writers have accredited to this nomad

---

[1] Besides the Assyrian books specifically mentioned in this Appendix, we have been indebted to Smith's "History of Babylonia" and "Assyria from the Earliest Times," Budge's "Babylonian Life and History," and Professor Sayce's "Fresh Light from the Ancient Monuments."

race the learning and civilization which they received from the Aryas. This should be borne in mind in reading the extracts relative to the early civilization of this locality, as obtained from Assyrian sources. "Accadian" is a provisional name given by Assyriologists to the nation or nations preceding the Semites, and should be held to designate the Aryan, as well as the Turanian, race.

During the reign of Sargon I., B.C. 3800 (the earliest monarch of the Semitic race yet known), the Turanian language had died out, or become nearly obsolete.

As all the learned works on astrology, astronomy, magic, the hymns and prayers, in fact, most of the literature of the people, were written in the Turanian tongue, the king ordered the priests to gather together from all the country the Turanian tablets and records, caused many of them to be copied, and others to be translated into the Semitic language, and gave directions for the completion of dictionaries, grammars, and vocabularies, to aid in the study and understanding of the language.

Professor Sayce, in "Assyria, its Princes, Priests, and People," says, "The Accadian standard work on astronomy, the 'Observations of Bell,' was compiled originally for the library of Sargon I. at Accad. It treated of various matters, — eclipses of the sun and moon, the conjunction of the sun and moon, the phases of Venus and Mars, the position of the polestar, the changes of the weather, the appearance of comets, and the like. . . . The immense collection of records of eclipses indicates the length of time during which observations of the heavens had been carried on. As it is generally stated whether a solar eclipse had happened 'according to calculation' or 'contrary to calculation,' it is clear that the Babylonians were acquainted at an early date with the periodicity of eclipses of the sun."

Speaking of the cuneiform writing, he says, —

"The Accadians had been the inventors of the hieroglyphic, or pictorial, characters out of which the cuneiform characters had afterward grown. Writing begins with pictures, and the writing of the Babylonians formed no exception to the rule. The pictures were at first painted on the papyrus-leaves which grew in the marshes of the Euphrates; but as time went on, a new and more plentiful material came to be employed in the shape of clay. All that was needed was to impress it, while still wet, with the hieroglyphic pictures, and then dry it in the air. . . . When once the discovery was made, that clay could be employed as a writing material, it was quickly turned to good account. All Babylonia began to write on tablets of clay; and though papyrus continued to be used, it was reserved for what we should now term *editions de luxe*."

Professor George Smith, in his "History of Babylonia," says, "Accadian literature was very extensive, and the libraries with which the whole country was stocked were full of treatises on all the branches of knowledge" pursued by these ancient people. He credits them with "inventing the wonderful system of writing, called from the shape of the characters 'cuneiform,' or wedge-shaped."

The Babylonians, the immediate successors of the Accadians, he says, "originated our astronomical system. . . . Mathematics, measures of time and capacity, weights and scales, laws and government, and every thing known to ancient times, received study and attention; while the arts of building, sculpture, painting, gem-engraving, metal-work, weaving, and many others, made proportionate progress." . . . But "they had a religion of the lowest and most degrading kind, . . . which had a multitude of gods, who were supposed to bring about in an irregular and capricious manner all the changes in nature, and all the misfortunes which happened to the people."

Samuel Johnson, in his last work on "Oriental Religions," volume on Persia, in the chapter on Cuneiform Monuments of the Accadian and the Assyrian, says, —

"The primitive civilization of the Mesopotamian basin was not Semitic, but Turanian or Ugro-Finnic. This is now recognized by the best scholars, by Oppert, Sayce, Lenormant, Schrader. A race whose language is agglutinative, allied to the Finnic, Tartar, Etruscan, it may be, — at all events, to the Mongolian family, —

brought the earliest cuneiform writing to this region, composed its earliest annals, developed a system of magic out of which came the ascendency of the Chaldees, and laid the foundation of its mythology.

"The records of this primeval civilization, which was flourishing in Chaldæa at least forty centuries ago, and perhaps a thousand years earlier than that, have been carefully preserved. If the Semitic Assyrians who supplanted the 'Accad and Sumir' had done nothing else but translate their contents from the older language and cuneiform type to which they were committed into their own current writing and tongue, not only preserving the originals, but providing for their study the appliances of lexicon and grammar, and all with a scrupulous historic affection amounting to a filial piety, like that of the Chinese in these matters,— they would have entitled themselves to the lasting gratitude of mankind, and can never be charged with having lived to little purpose; and this they have thoroughly done.

"The records of the old Accadian kings, from Lig-Bagus of Ur down, are jejune, — mere items of temple and tower building, their names now given in Semitic, now in Turanian. But their literature was preserved in libraries located in the numerous cities of Babylonia; and from these the Semitic Assyrians not only brought the great works of poetry, mythology, science, and magic, which they translated and studied so carefully, but also probably derived their own system of free public libraries, like those of Sargon and Asshur-banipal, into the inner working of which we can look to-day with astonishment that there is nothing new under the sun. The literary capacity of these old Turanians is perhaps the most remarkable fact in history. The oldest of epics, to which the name of Izdubar has been provisionally given, is an elaborated product of Accadian genius, forty centuries old, and shows how early the poetic faculty of man found inspiration in the great lights of heaven. This marvellous epic, with its twelve great legends based on the twelve zodiacal signs, turning their Accadian names into dramatic personifications, and the process of the sun through their successive mansions into labors of a mythic hero, which are curiously paralleled or repeated in the Semitic and Aryan forms of the Hercules myth; interweaving also the lunar phases in a form which is the prototype of that wide-spread cycle of myths wherein a dying god is mourned by the spirit of love in Nature, and sought by her in the under-world, — the marvellous epic is worthy to be called the cradle of mythologies, even from what we already know of its contents. . . . .

"The most characteristic thing about Accadian civilization is the passion for literature. In its old deluge myth, as reported by the Greeks from Berosus, the Chaldæan Noah (Xisuthrus) is bidden to bury the sacred writings at Sippara, his native city, before the flood comes; and there, after he has been taken up to heaven, his followers return to recover them.

Oannes, the fish-god from the seacoast to whom these primitive Chaldæans ascribe their culture, is expressly said to have brought them letters. . . .

"The Assyrians who transmitted this Turanian wisdom illustrate the same laws. Their respectful heed to it and their patient care for its preservation by grammatical researches, syllabaries, lists of corresponding words, was a recognition of universal relations, an escape from race-prejudice, surprising at so early a period. It seems to lay the corner-stone of a cosmopolitanism which has since conditioned the progress of civilization. . . .

"It is difficult as yet to determine how large a portion of Assyrian culture was derived from Accadian sources. The development was certainly continuous, and even without the light thrown on it by cuneiform studies is clearly traceable to the seacoast at the mouth of the Euphrates. It is here that all ancient tradition places the earliest social, industrial, intellectual life of Western Asia. Hither, as Berosus reports from Babylonian records, came the mythic civilizers, Oannes and his Annedoti, — half fish, half man, — at repeated intervals, to teach rude men the arts of life."

Assurbanipal (B.C. 648 to 626), one of the greatest of Assyrian kings, caused the ancient tablets yet remaining to be collected together from all parts of the country, and deposited in his library at Nineveh. He ordered numerous copies to be made of all the valuable documents, and every care taken to preserve to future generations the knowledge therein contained.

In the destruction of Nineveh, these literary treasures, being in brick rooms or vaults, were covered by the *débris* of the fallen walls of the building; and there they remained until the excavations of Layard and others revealed them to our eyes.

The dictionaries, grammars, and vocabularies prepared by Sargon I. fifty-six hundred years ago have enabled the Assyrian scholars of the present day to obtain a knowledge of the Turanian tongue, which would otherwise have been impossible.

www.ingramcontent.com/pod-product-compliance
Lightning Source LLC
Chambersburg PA
CBHW022026240426
43667CB00042B/1200